WBI DEVELOPMENT STUDIES

Japan, Moving Toward a More Advanced Knowledge Economy

Volume 2: *Advanced Knowledge-Creating Companies*

Edited by
Hirotaka Takeuchi
Tsutomu Shibata

The World Bank
Washington, D.C.

ISBN 0-8213-6674-2

Library of Congress cataloging-in-publication data has been applied for.

Contents

Figures

Tables

Boxes

Foreword

Knowledge has long been recognized as a key source of economic growth and a valuable asset that can be leveraged, especially now in an era of increasing globalization. As a result of deeper integration among economies and fueled by the revolutionary advances in information technology (IT), the supply of and demand for knowledge and its application have led to significant challenges as well as opportunities for both developing and developed countries. To create and sustain an effective knowledge economy, countries and companies worldwide must become more knowledge-competitive. This book analyzes Japan as a knowledge economy, with a view to providing lessons for the developing world.

Japan's rapid economic recovery after World War II, assisted by imported technology, was indeed remarkable. In the mid-1960s, it was the second largest World Bank borrower, while only two decades later it was the second largest contributor. Already in the mid-1960s, Japan's GDP was beginning to catch up with some of the European economies.

In the 1970s and 1980s, Japan was held up as a model of economic growth for developing countries; and in the 1980s, companies in the industrial countries realized that they could also learn a great deal from Japanese firms. Some analysts even believed that Japan would dominate the world economy in most major industries because of its advanced production system. Then, in the 1990s, a long period of economic stagnation, especially relative to the resurgence of IT companies in the United States, led many to dismiss Japan as an important source of ideas.

These polar opposite perceptions, however, do not reflect the real Japanese economy past or present. The earlier positive assessments ignored the existence of a substantial number of uncompetitive industries, while the more recent dismissals ignore some highly competitive companies and industries. This book provides a more balanced account. In particular, it assesses Japan's status as a knowledge-based economy, applying the "four-pillar" analysis developed by the World Bank Institute (WBI), and highlights the success of several knowledge-advanced Japanese companies.

In mid-2006, the Japanese economy appears to be emerging from a lengthy stagnation. Japan has been a source of global best practices in both manufacturing processes and management; and although many of its characteristic large-firm management approaches may seem ill-suited to the evolving global economy, others have been adapted and continue to be on the cutting edge. On a macro level, Japan has become the world's second largest economy and has a very high level of social equity.

At the same time, Japan is facing many challenges as it moves into a more advanced position in the global knowledge economy, including the need for a more flexible labor market, and the provision of risk capital, safety nets, and lifelong learning. Some of these issues are also relevant to developing countries.

Among the achievements that modern Japan can be proud of is its economic growth with equity. Knowledge was a crucial tool in this process. What has worked in the past may not work in the future or in other countries, but it is nevertheless important to understand the underlying factors and dynamics. We hope that readers from advanced knowledge-based economies as well as those aspiring to higher levels of knowledge competitiveness will find the lessons and insights in this book useful.

Frannie A. Léautier
Vice President and Head
World Bank Institute

Authors' Contact Information

Tatsuji Hayakawa
Consultant
World Bank Institute
E-mail: thayakawa@worldbank.org

Kazuo Ichijo
Professor
Graduate School of Social Sciences, Hitotsubashi University
E-mail: ichijo@qf7.so-net.ne.jp

Reiko Kosugi
Assistant Research Director
The Japan Institute for Labour Policy and Training
E-mail: rkosu@jil.go.jp

Ken Kusunoki
Associate Professor
Graduate School of International Corporate Strategy, Hitotsubashi University
E-mail: kkusunoki@ics.hit-u.ac.jp

Hideaki Miyajima
Professor
Graduate School of Commerce, Waseda University
E-mail: miyajima@waseda.jp

Kazuyuki Motohashi
Professor
Research Center for Advanced Science and Technology, University of Tokyo
E-mail: motohashi-kazuyuki@rieti.go.jp

Risaburo Nezu
Senior Managing Director
Fujitsu Research Institute
E-mail: nezurisa@fri.fujitsu.com

Ikujiro Nonaka
Professor
Graduate School of International Corporate Strategy, Hitotsubashi University
E-mail: inonaka@ics.hit-u.ac.jp

Hiroyuki Odagiri
Professor
Graduate School of Economics, Hitotsubashi University
E-mail: odagiri@econ.hit-u.ac.jp

Emi Osono
Associate Professor
Graduate School of International Corporate Strategy, Hitotsubashi University
E-mail: osono@ics.hit-u.ac.jp

Tsutomu Shibata
Senior Adviser
World Bank Institute
E-mail: tshibata@worldbank.org

Hirotaka Takeuchi
Dean
Graduate School of International Corporate Strategy, Hitotsubashi University
E-mail: htakeuchi@ics.hit-u.ac.jp

Akiyoshi Yonezawa
Associate Professor
Faculty of University Evaluation and Research, National Institution for Academic
Degrees and University Evaluation
E-mail: yonezawa@niad.ac.jp

Glossary

Currency Equivalents

Exchange rate effective March 31, 2006
Currency unit = yen (JPY)

US$	1.00 = 117.8 JPY
JPY	1.00 = US$0.0085

Fiscal year   April 1–March 31

All dollar amounts in this book are U.S. dollars, unless otherwise noted.

Abbreviations

ATM	Automatic teller machine
CRT	Cathode ray tube
ICT	Information and communication technology
IT	Information technology
IY	Ito-Yokado Co, Ltd. [from 2005, part of Seven & I Holdings Co.]
JICA	Japan International Cooperation Agency
LCD	Liquid crystal display [flat-panel screen]
NIH	"not invented here" syndrome
OTJ	On-the-job [training]
PC	Personal computer
PDA	Personal digital assistant
POS	Point-of-sale [information system]
SCM	Supply-chain management
SECI	Socialization, externalization, combination, and internalization process
SEJ	Seven-Eleven Japan Co., Ltd. [from 2005, part of Seven & I Holdings Co.]
SKU	Stockkeeping units
TMS	Toyota Motor Sales
WTP	Willingness to pay

Japanese Terms

Burabura sha-in	"Walking-around employees"
Genchi genbutsu	"Go see the actual article at the scene." Similar to "management by walking around," but with more emphasis on *understanding* on the part of the managers as part of their conscious problem-finding and problem-solving process.
Kaizen	Continuous improvement
Kanban	Just-in-time [inventory system]

1

The New Dynamism of the Knowledge-Creating Company

Hirotaka Takeuchi

To be on the cutting edge in a knowledge economy, a company must be knowledge-creating. Being simply knowledgeable is not enough. What does it mean to be a knowledge-creating company? As described below, the concepts are straight-forward—it is the practice that is hard. The first detailed analysis was published in 1995 by Nonaka and Takeuchi in a study titled *The Knowledge-Creating Company: How Japanese Companies Create the Dynamics of Innovation.* Subsequently, the knowl-edge movement has spread and the literature grown enormously.[1]

How could a book written in Japan about Japanese companies spawn such a fol-lowing and follow-up? The short answer is because there was something to learn from the Japanese approach to knowledge. But that was the past; the distinctive fea-tures of the Japanese approach to knowledge described in 1995 are now well known.

What of the future? Are Japanese firms still innovative? Is the Japanese approach to knowledge creation still at the frontier of management? Has a new dynamism propelled it even further? Or has the Japanese approach been overtaken and thus reached a stalemate?

As one of the authors of the original study, I have joined the World Bank Insti-tute and colleagues at Hitotsubashi University to produce this volume to answer these questions. The short answers are innovation is alive and well in Japan, and the Japanese approach has a new dynamism that makes it as relevant as ever—perhaps even more so.

The short answers are elaborated in the five chapters that follow. These are case studies of Seven-Eleven Japan, Lexus Division of Toyota, Sharp, Keyence, Nintendo,

---

1. Throughout the world there are trade associations and journals bent on advancing best practices in knowledge management. (Important publications in the field include the *Journal of Knowledge Management, Knowledge and Process Management,* and *Journal of Intellectual Capital.*)

Many firms now have a chief knowledge officer or a knowledge creation department. Governments have joined as well, sending officers to overseas conferences and training programs. (As an example, in October 2004 and October 2005, the Hitotsubashi University Graduate School of International Corporate Strategy (ICS) hosted two-week seminars on knowledge management in Tokyo for 18 high-ranking government officials representing 12 countries from Asia. The seminar was funded by the Japan International Cooperation Agency (JICA) and directed by Ikujiro Nonaka. It consisted of lectures, case studies, and company visits.)

There are even endowed professorships, including the Xerox Distinguished Faculty in Knowledge at the University of California, Berkeley (a chair held by Nonaka since it was cre-ated in 1997).

and Shimano. These firms span a wide variety of industry segments, including retailing (convenience stores), automobiles, television, electronic components, home video games, and bicycle parts. They are the target of investigation because they have leading shares in their market segments and have been especially good at continuous innovation and self-renewal. (Japan does have failures, and something can be learned from them as well, as shown in chapter 3 of the project's companion volume, *Japan, Moving Toward a More Advanced Knowledge Economy: Assessment and Lessons.*)

The next section briefly summarizes the case studies. The remaining sections summarize the concepts that make up the Japanese approach to knowledge.

The Case Studies

The experiences of the Japanese companies discussed in this volume suggest a fresh way of thinking about competitiveness within the knowledge economy. This section provides an overview of how the companies studied have achieved breakthroughs in innovation and knowledge creation.

Convenience stores were a U.S. innovation that has been radically improved in Japan. Indeed, Seven-Eleven Japan (SEJ) has gone from being the local franchisee to owner of the original U.S. company. SEJ is known not only for its innovative products (such as gourmet rice balls, exotic salads, noodles from famous restaurants, and local delicacies targeted to specific geographic regions) and services (such as mobile phone recharging, dry cleaning dropoff, online shopping pickup, banking, voter registration, and parcel delivery), but also for a novel business model. It has created new markets where none existed, and changed the way people live and work in Japan. To do this, the company has worked closely with suppliers and customers, as well as service providers.

Lexus became the top-selling car in the U.S. luxury car segment in 2000, surpassing Mercedes Benz just 11 years after being introduced. Through a process called *kaizen* ("continuous improvement"), Toyota relentlessly found ways to improve its production system, quality, and productivity to produce "the finest car ever built." Lexus's innovation, however, is not merely about coming up with a breakthrough product. It is equally about continuous innovation in building its coveted customer relationship program. It never stops hammering away at problems and opportunities in its interaction with customers.

Many electronics products have become commodities. To avoid the low margins this implies, firms have sought to move from "dimensional" competition to "non-dimensional" competition. Keyence, the leading sensor and measuring equipment manufacturer in Japan, seeks to make this move by working very closely with its customers to solve their individual problems and offer customized solutions. Nintendo, the leading producer of home-use game players in the world, is peering over the shoulders of those playing games to find out the "fun" element they are seeking. These two companies have discovered that tapping their own customers can lead to breakthroughs in innovation.

Sharp became one of the world's leading producers of liquid crystal display (LCD) television sets by relentlessly pursuing serial innovation through a process of creating, sharing, protecting, and discarding knowledge. Sharp, a pioneer in LCDs since the 1970s, was the first to open a sixth-generation fabrication plant, which means it can make LCD panels as large as 1,500 mm by 1,800 mm (known as *tatami*-size in Japan). Katsuhiko Machida, only two months after becoming president in 1998, set the goal of all Sharp televisions sold in the domestic market being flat-screen LCD sets by 2005. By then, the company no longer produced tube televisions for the Japanese market. As Machida has shown, one way to spur innovation is being willing to think big and tackle a goal others deem too risky.

Shimano has a 90% share of parts for higher-end bikes sold by the top-three brands in the United States (Trek, Giant, and Specialized) and a dominant worldwide position in parts for mountain bikes. Shimano triggered breakthroughs in innovation by knocking down walls between research, manufacturing, and marketing. Outside the company, it has fueled continuous innovation by working closely with its customers. Every year, Shimano dispatches more than a dozen employees of various backgrounds to work with manufacturers and retailers in the United States and Europe for several months to gauge consumer trends. In addition, its top management team regularly meets top racers, such as Tour de France winner Lance Armstrong, to discuss products and prototypes.

The Japanese Approach to Knowledge

The Japanese approach to knowledge differs from the traditional Western approach in a number of key areas. The distinctiveness of the Japanese approach is summarized in Table 1.1.

Company Viewed as a Living Organism

In the dominant Western philosophy, the individual is the principal agent who possesses and processes knowledge. The Japanese approach also recognizes that knowledge begins with the individual. At the same time, however, it recognizes the important role the interaction between the individual and the company plays in creating organizational knowledge, as well as the important role the group plays in facilitating this interaction.

Thus, knowledge creation takes place at three levels:

* the individual,
* the group, and
* the organizational levels within the company.

The difference in how a company is viewed affects the knowledge creation process. Deeply ingrained in the traditions of Western management, from Frederick Taylor to Herbert Simon, is a view of the company as a *machine* for "processing information." In Japan, a company is viewed more as a living organism. Much like

Table 1.1.   The Japanese Approach to Knowledge

1.   Views a company as a living organism, rather than as a machine;
2.   Focuses on justifying belief much more than on seeking truth;
3.   Emphasizes tacit knowledge over explicit knowledge;
4.   Relies on self-organizing teams, not just existing organizational structures, to create new knowledge;
5.   Turns to middle managers to resolve contradictions between top management and front-line workers; and
6.   Acquires knowledge from outsiders as well as insiders.

an individual, a company can have a collective sense of identity and fundamental purpose. A shared understanding of what the company stands for (mission), where it is going (vision), what kind of world it wants to live in (values), and, most important, how to make that world a reality, lie at the base of Japanese thinking.

In this respect, knowledge creation is as much about ideals as it is about ideas. Ideals fuel innovation within a knowledge-creating company. The essence of innovation is to re-create the world according to a particular mission, vision, or value. To create new knowledge means quite literally to re-create the company, and all the individuals in it, in a nonstop process of personal and organizational self-renewal. In the knowledge-creating company, creating new knowledge is a way of behaving—indeed, a way of being—in which everyone is a knowledge worker. This contrasts with knowledge creation viewed as a specialized function or the activity of a specialized department. (For more on this topic, see Nonaka and Takeuchi 1995, ch. 3 and Nonaka 1994.)

Knowledge as Justified Belief

Most Western philosophers agree that knowledge is "justified true belief," a concept introduced by Plato. Traditional Western epistemology (theory of knowledge) has focused on "truthfulness" as the essential attribute of knowledge. As a result, it emphasizes the absolute, static, and nonhuman nature of knowledge, typically expressed in propositions and formal logic. Consider, for example, mathematics, in which absolute truth is deduced from rational reasoning grounded in axioms. Or consider, for example, the formal logic of deduction: All humans are mortal; Socrates is human; therefore, Socrates is mortal. All the statements are logical, but they leave little room for new thought to emerge.

The Japanese approach, on the other hand, highlights the nature of knowledge as "justified belief." It emphasizes the nature of knowledge as a dynamic human process of justifying personal belief toward "the truth." It takes the view that knowledge is essentially related to human action. It also focuses attention on the active, subjective nature of knowledge represented by such terms as "belief" and "commitment" that are deeply rooted in the personal value system of an individual.

The Japanese approach clarifies the distinction between information and knowledge. Both are about *meaning.* They are context-specific and relational. However, they differ in two respects. First, unlike information, knowledge is about action. It is always knowledge "to some end." Second, unlike information, knowledge is about belief and commitment. Knowledge is a function of a particular stance, perspective, or intention. Because knowledge emerges out of subjective views of the world, it probably cannot reach the "one and only absolute truth." Hence, the Japanese approach is more pragmatic, regarding knowledge temporarily as "truth" as long as it is practical to those who use it. (For more discussion of what knowledge is, see Nonaka and Takeuchi 1995, ch. 2.)

Emphasis on Tacit Knowledge

The traditions of Western management view knowledge as *explicit*—something formal and systematic. Explicit knowledge can be expressed in words and numbers, and easily communicated and shared in the form of data, scientific formulas, or codified procedures. Thus, anything digital, anything that can easily be processed by a computer, transmitted electronically, or stored in databases is routinely equated with knowledge.

Japanese companies have a very different understanding of knowledge. They recognize that the knowledge expressed in words and numbers represents only the tip of the iceberg. They view knowledge as being primarily *tacit*—something not easily visible and expressible. Tacit knowledge is highly personal and hard to formalize, making it difficult to communicate or to share with others. This is why Japanese often resort to figurative language, metaphors, and analogies. Subjective insights, intuitions, and hunches fall in this category of knowledge. Furthermore, tacit knowledge is deeply rooted in an individual's action and experience, as well as in the ideals, beliefs, values, or emotions a person embraces.

Managers in Japan emphasize the importance of learning from direct experience, as well as through trial and error. Like a child learning to eat, walk, and talk, they learn with their *bodies,* not just with their *minds*. This tradition of emphasizing the "oneness of body and mind" has been a unique feature of Japanese thinking since Zen Buddhism became established in the 13th century. It is the ultimate ideal condition that Zen practitioners seek by means of internal meditation and disciplined life.

Zen profoundly affected samurai education, which sought to develop wisdom through physical training. Being a "man of action" was considered more important than mastering philosophy and literature. Learning from direct experience stands in stark contrast to "systems thinking," which focuses on learning with the mind. Thus, Senge (1990), the apostle of systems thinking and the learning organization, says trial-and-error learning is a delusion, as most critical decisions made in an organization have systemwide consequences stretching over years and decades, a time frame that makes learning from direct experience an impossibility.

Self-Organizing Teams

Self-organizing teams play a central role in the Japanese approach to knowledge creation. They provide a shared context in which individuals can carry on a dialogue, something that may involve considerable conflict and disagreement. It is precisely such contradiction that pushes individuals to question existing premises and to make sense of their experiences in a new way. This kind of dynamic interaction at the group level facilitates the conversion of personal knowledge into organizational knowledge.

A key aspect of the teams is that they are made up of members from different functions, departments, and divisions within the company. As an example, at Sharp, employees can be uprooted from any division or rank in the company at any time to work on an urgent project for as long as two years. This reflects the fact that no one department or group of experts has exclusive responsibility for creating new knowledge.

Central Role of Middle Managers

Middle managers play a key role in the Japanese approach to organizational knowledge creation. Top management provides a sense of direction regarding where the company should be headed and articulates that vision or dream ("what ought to be") for the company, while frontline workers in the trenches look at reality ("what is"). The role of middle managers is to resolve any contradictions between what top management hopes to create and what actually exists in the real world by creating mid-range business and product concepts. This approach to knowledge creation is called the *middle-up-down* management process.

That middle managers serve as the bridge between top management and front-line workers is a commonplace. However, in the United States, in particular, the bridge came to be seen as a bottleneck. Consequently, as firms sought to become "lean and mean" in the 1980s and 1990s, middle management positions were often eliminated. The negative consequences of this downsizing are now being felt, and new attention is being paid to the important, positive, synthesizing role of middle managers. The Japanese approach to knowledge creation and organizational structure has always recognized their centrality.

By virtue of being positioned at the intersection of the vertical and horizontal flows of information in the company, middle managers have access to a lot of knowledge. This makes them ideal candidates to lead project teams. As such, they are able to remake reality according to the company's vision.

To become team leaders in the knowledge economy, middle managers must meet a number of qualifications. They need to be skilled at

1. coming up with hypotheses in order to create mid-range concepts,
2. integrating various methodologies for knowledge creation,
3. encouraging dialogue among team members,
4. using metaphors and analogies in order to help others generate and articulate imagination,
5. engendering trust among team members,
6. envisioning the future course of action based on an understanding of the past, and
7. coordinating and managing projects.

Acquiring Knowledge from Outside

Japanese companies have continually turned to their suppliers, customers, dealers, local communities, and even competitors for insights and clues. Knowledge acquired from the outside is shared widely within the company, stored as part of the company's knowledge base, and utilized by those engaged in new developing technologies, products, systems, or ways of competing.

A classic example is Ikuko Tanaka apprenticing with a master breadmaker for several months to gain the insight needed to overcome problems with the automatic bread-making machine Matsushita was developing. Toyota is the archetypical company that works closely with its group of affiliated suppliers to create knowledge across organizational boundaries.

The Modes of Knowledge Conversion

Knowledge creation moves through four modes of knowledge conversion, known as the SECI (socialization, externalization, combination, and internalization) process. This is shown in Table 1.2 and Figure 1.1.

Moving through the spiral, the interaction between tacit and explicit knowledge is amplified. The spiral becomes larger in scale as it moves up the ontological levels

Table 1.2.　*The SECI Spiral*

Socialization	Sharing and creating tacit knowledge through direct experience
Externalization	Articulating tacit knowledge through dialogue and reflection
Combination	Systematizing and applying explicit knowledge and information
Internalization	Learning and acquiring new tacit knowledge in practice

Figure 1.1.　*SECI Process of Knowledge Spiral*

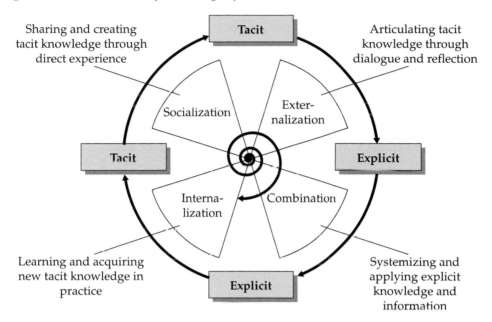

Source: Adapted from Nonaka and Takeuchi (1995).

(that is, individual, group, organizational, and interorganizational). Knowledge created through the SECI process triggers a new spiral of knowledge creation, expanding horizontally and vertically as it transcends sectional, departmental, divisional, and even organizational boundaries. As the spiral expands beyond organizational boundaries, knowledge created by universities, suppliers, customers, competitors, local communities, government, and others interacts with each other in amplifying the knowledge-creating process. (See Ahmadjian 2004 for a more detailed description.)

To create a knowledge spiral, a number of different conversions or syntheses need to take place. These include a conversion or synthesis across

1. tacit knowledge and explicit knowledge,
2. levels (individual, group, and organizational) *within* the company,
3. functions, departments, and divisions *within* the company,
4. layers (top-management, middle manager, and front-line worker) *within* the company,
5. knowledge *inside* the company and knowledge *outside* the company created by suppliers, customers, dealers, local communities, competitors, universities, government and other stakeholders.

These synthesizing capabilities make or break the knowledge creation process.

The Concept of *Ba*

To explain the interactions involved in knowledge creation, the concept of *ba* is used. *Ba* describes the "linkage points" of interactions and "where" they take place, as well as "when" and "how" (relationships). As such, *ba* can be interpreted as a type of nexus. But *ba* is much more than a simple nexus: A *ba* provides a shared context in which individuals can interact with each other to create new meaning.

By its nature, a *ba* is ad hoc and dynamic. This makes it more analogous to improvisation in jazz than to a scored musical work. When jazz is being improvised, contexts are shared in real time, whereas when an orchestra is performing, contexts are pretty much shared in advance. Note that ad hoc is not the same as spontaneously formed: an organization can establish a linkage point and designate a space that may then become a *ba.* Table 1.3 summarizes the basic characteristics of *ba.*

Table 1.3.   *Basic Characteristics of* Ba

Linkage points[1]
Physical group: Conventions and symposiums, academic and industry associations, internal meetings, project teams and task forces, etc.
Conceptual group: Communities of practice, etc.

Where[1]
Physical space: A convention center, factory floor, shop floor, office space, meeting room, etc.
Virtual space: Teleconferences, file sharing, social networking services, chat rooms and online exchanges such as blogs, and group-edited sites such as wikis, etc.

Nature
Ad hoc and dynamic.
Shared context.
Existential (having "being" in time and space).

Types
Internal (that is, within an organization, etc.).
External with customers.
External with noncustomers (such as suppliers, dealers, competitors, local communities, and governments).

1. A *ba* can involve multiple linkages and "wheres." The lists are intended to be indicative of the possibilities.

Conclusion

To state the book's conclusion upfront, the next five chapters should convince the reader that a new dynamism is in play in how Japanese companies create the dynamics of innovation. Japanese companies are pushing the frontier of knowledge management even further, generating a myriad of new concepts. More important, they have shown that the key to gaining competitive advantage in a knowledge economy lies at the *interorganizational* level. The new dynamism comes from finding ways to work together with outsiders—customers, suppliers, dealers, and even competitors—to create new knowledge. New knowledge—whether from *inside* or *outside*—fuels innovative breakthroughs.

The bar has been raised. By the mid-1990s, it was clear that companies could benefit from using the Japanese approach to organizational knowledge creation. The Japanese approach has been evolving. Now, any company wanting to compete on knowledge must learn from the Japanese approach to *interorganizational* knowledge creation.

References

Ahmadjian, Christina L. 2004. "Inter-organizational Knowledge Creation: Knowledge and Networks." In Hirotaka Takeuchi and Ikujiro Nonaka, editors, *Hitotsubashi on Knowledge Management.* Singapore: John Wiley & Sons (Asia).

Nonaka, Ikujiro. 1991. "The Knowledge-Creating Company." *Harvard Business Review,* Nov–Dec.

Nonaka, Ikujiro. 1994. "A Dynamic Theory of Organizational Knowledge Creation." *Organizational Science* 5 (1): 14–37.

Nonaka, Ikujiro, and Hirotaka Takeuchi. 1995. *The Knowledge-Creating Company: How Japanese Companies Create the Dynamics of Innovation.* Oxford University Press.

Senge, P.M. 1990. *The Fifth Disclipline: The Age and Practice of the Learning Organization.* Century Business.

Takeuchi, Hirotaka. 1998. "Beyond Knowledge Management: Lessons from Japan." *Monash Mt Eliza Business Journal* 1.

2

Knowledge Creation in the Convenience Store Industry: Seven-Eleven Japan

Ikujiro Nonaka

Society has gradually turned into a knowledge society. Reflecting societal changes, the concepts of knowledge and its management have become popular in management literature and business magazines. The aim of this chapter is the further understanding of the role of knowledge creation as a competitive advantage in convenience store networks. In particular, Seven-Eleven Japan (SEJ) is examined from the perspective of a knowledge-based theory of the firm (Nonaka 1991, 1994; Nonaka and Takeuchi 1995; Nonaka and Toyama 2002; Takeuchi and Nonaka 2004; Nonaka and Toyama 2003).

SEJ is Japan's largest convenience store chain, with more than 10,000 outlets, and one of the most profitable firms in Japan. The company has a knowledge-creating system that utilizes and systematizes tacit knowledge from customers to create products and services that enable SEJ to fulfill evolving customer needs and wants more efficiently than its main competitors.

The chapter is organized as follows. The next section lays out the conceptual framework in which the components of knowledge-creating companies are explained through interlocking ontology and epistemology. Knowledge creation at SEJ is then described through knowledge vision, driving objectives, dialogues, practices, *ba* (meaning a "shared context in motion"), and external networks. SEJ's international operations are also discussed. The primary components of SEJ's success are then analyzed. The conclusion includes managerial implications.

Conceptual Framework

The knowledge-based firm can be explained by two interlocking components. Knowledge vision, driving objectives, dialogues, and practices are the basic components of a knowledge-creating firm. The knowledge creation process is context-specific and dependent on the shared context of interaction (*ba*). Knowledge is created at the individual, group, organizational, and interorganizational levels through the interaction between tacit and explicit knowledge as well as the agents and environment. Tacit and explicit knowledge are not totally separable, but rather can be understood as mutually complementary entities. Although tacit knowledge is personal, hard to externalize, and context-specific (Polanyi 1952), explicit knowledge is codifiable and transferable.

Basic Components of the Knowledge-Creating Firm

The basic components of the knowledge-creating firm are knowledge visions, driving objectives, dialogues, and practices (Figure 2.1).

Figure 2.1.   *Basic Components of the Knowledge-Creating Firm*

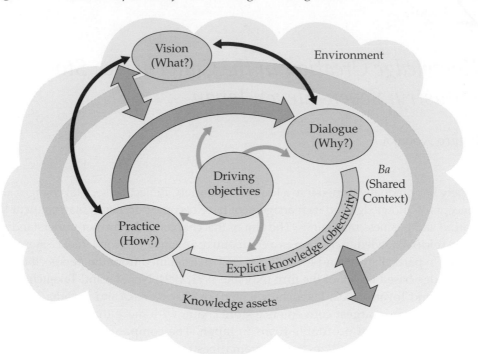

Knowledge vision, which determines a firm's ideal mission and domain, is rooted in the question of "what does a company exist for?" In contrast with analytical strategies, knowledge vision is a value-driven articulation of an idealistic praxis for a company. Philosopher Martin Heidegger (1962) proposed that the most important dimension of temporality is the future, as it presents the potentiality-for-being.

A combination of past experiences and projected future give rise to present action. Similarly, managers in strategic decision making need to constantly look back, attending to the products and processes of the past, while also gazing forward in the process of creating knowledge. Knowledge visions thus form a nexus between the past, present, and future as the past has meaning only as a projection of the future. Middle managers bridge top-management visions with the chaotic reality at the front line. They internalize visions through interactions with top managers, and take the roles of instructor, coach, mentor, and coordinator to facilitate knowledge creation.

Driving objectives, which are actualized in concepts, numbers, as well as collective discipline, orchestrate the knowledge visions, dialogues, and practices into a dynamic coherence (Nonaka, Peltokorpi, and Tomae 2005). This connecting link is furnished by the simple fact that a self-actualizing action needs to be tied to future aspirations and the surrounding reality. That is, companies need to generate profits to provide resources for knowledge creation. Management can facilitate insights in companies with a single economic denominator or a principle to embrace market knowledge for anticipation of emerging customer demand (see Collins 2001). These economic denominators can be subtle, sometimes to the point of transparency, in letting the reality emerge through reflection and social interaction.

Dialogues enhance co-understanding by linking various *ba* within and beyond the firm's boundaries. To create a free flow of ideas, dialogues should be based on empathy, reciprocity, involvement, and openness. Actors need to express their subjective feelings and suspend their prejudices to view the phenomena from multiple angles at the same time (Depraz, Varela, and Vermersch 2003). A stream of open-meaning flows provides a space in which the participants can reflect the functioning of feelings, beliefs, ideas, and thought. Dialectics of language, therefore, is more than the logical verbalization of thoughts in which no middle point exists between the two propositions.

Practices are "dialectics in action" processes in which people reflect the acquired tacit knowledge and skills based on self-transcending action. Part of the action is inherently tacit, so practices deviate from organizational routines as the collective capacity to perform recognizable patterns of action (Nelson and Winter 1982). Practices can be equated with the traditional Japanese *kata*, the ideal style of action and practice composed of a continuous cycle of learning (*shu*) ⇒ breaking (*ha*) ⇒ creating (*ri*). People can achieve the ideal form by reflection either through practical involvement or by temporal suspension in action (Heidegger 1962; Shön 1983). Once practices are shared and systematized, they become a part of the company's knowledge assets.

Ba is a shared context in motion in which knowledge is shared, created, and utilized (Nonaka and Konno 1998). The essence of *ba* is the context and the meanings that are shared and created through interactions that occur in a specific time, space, and history, rather than in a space itself. *Ba* can emerge in individuals, working groups, project teams, informal circles, meetings, virtual space, and customer contact.

Participating in *ba* means becoming involved and transcending one's own limited perspectives. Japanese philosopher Kitaro Nishida (1921/1990) stated that the essence of *ba* is "nothingness." Within *ba*, one can be open to others by forgetting oneself, that is, one's preconceived notion of what is absolutely true for oneself. One can see oneself through this process in relation to others, and accept others' views and values so that subjective views are understood and shared. Leaders can energize *ba* by providing physical space (for example, meeting rooms), cyberspace (computer networks), and mental space (common goals). Organizational structures and management systems (career systems and franchising systems) also energize *ba*.

The Knowledge Creation Process

Knowledge is created through the continuous conversion of tacit knowledge and explicit knowledge (Nonaka 1991, 1994; Nonaka and Takeuchi 1995). The knowledge creation process takes place through four phases of knowledge conversion.

1. *Socialization* (a process in which new tacit knowledge is formed from old tacit knowledge) ⇒
2. *Externalization* (a process in which new explicit knowledge is formed from new tacit knowledge) ⇒
3. *Combination* (a process in which new tacit knowledge is formed from old explicit knowledge) ⇒
4. *Internalization* (a process in which new knowledge is formed from new explicit knowledge).

The process starts with socialization, which is the converting of new tacit knowledge through shared experiences in daily social interactions. During this phase, the phenomenological method of accepting, seeing, and feeling things as they are is effective. The phenomenological and Eastern philosophical concepts of temporary suspension of all personal biases, beliefs, and preconceptions enable pure experience that can be acquired and shared (Nishida 1921/1990; Husserl 1931).

People in the externalization phase share their tacit knowledge through metaphors, analogies, models, dialogues, and reflection. This phase is founded on idealism, as tacit knowledge is articulated by pursuing the essence or ideal of one's subjective experience. To externalize deeper layers of personal knowledge, a sequential use of the methods of abduction and retroduction are effective (Lawson 1997). Important enablers in this phase are love, care, trust, the embracing of paradoxes, and the cultivation of opposite traits (Nonaka and Takeuchi 1995).

During the combination phase, the externalized tacit knowledge is systemized and crystallized in explicit forms for collective awareness and practical use. Here, contradictions are solved mostly through logic. Rationalism is an effective method to combine, edit, and break down explicit knowledge. Knowledge combination can be facilitated by information technology, division of labor, and hierarchy. The creative use of computer networks and databases helps to transfer explicit knowledge within and beyond the firm's boundaries.

New explicit knowledge during the internalization phase is acquired through soft experimentations and discipline. The pragmatism of learning by doing is an effective method to test, modify, and embody the explicit knowledge as one's own knowledge. The concepts and products, as the end product of knowledge creation, drive profits and shareholder value through profitable growth. The process enables firms to accumulate intellectual resources or knowledge assets.

Knowledge creation is an upward spiral in which the interaction between tacit and explicit knowledge is amplified through the four modes of knowledge conversion. The spiral, following the knowledge visions, becomes larger as it moves up the ontological levels. This process can trigger new spirals of knowledge creation, expanding horizontally and vertically as it moves through communities of interaction, transcending sectional, departmental, divisional, and even organizational boundaries.

SEJ

SEJ is the leading convenience store chain in Japan. Total store sales were ¥2.4 trillion, and operating revenue was ¥467 billion, for the year ending February 2005. The number of outlets in Japan stood at 10,826, having passed 10,000 in 2003. SEJ had a 31.5% share in sales and 21.7% of the stores. Average daily sales per store were ¥647,000. Equivalent per store sales of major rivals were ¥484,000 for Lawson Inc and ¥464,000 for Familymart Co. Ltd. Even larger differences can be detected in consolidated operating income, which were ¥165,698 million for SEJ, ¥38,087 million for Lawson, and ¥29,092 million for Familymart.

Most SEJ outlets are franchises, but the company directly managed 3,218 company-owned stores at the end of fiscal 2004. The average store in Japan is only about 110 square meters (just under 1,200 square feet), about half the size of Seven-Eleven stores in the United States. With the size limitation, the typical store can carry only 3,000 stockkeeping units (SKUs) at a time, compared with the over 100,000 a large supermarket will have. (An SKU is a unique product as regards manufacturer and such characteristics as size, color, flavor, and the like.)

Sales in Seven-Eleven stores can be classified into processed foods such as drinks, noodles, bread, and snacks; fast foods such as rice balls, box lunches, and hamburgers; fresh foods such as milk and dairy products; and nonfood items such as magazines, ladies' stockings, and batteries. Box 2.1 provides further background.

Box 2.1.   *The Relationship between SEJ and Ito-Yokado*

In 1973 the Southland Corporation, based in the United States, licensed Ito-Yokado Co., Ltd. (IY) to develop the Seven-Eleven convenience store concept in Japan. Since opening the first store in Tokyo in May 1974 and being publicly listed five years later, SEJ has been one of the most profitable companies in Japan. Ultimately, SEJ became larger than its parent. As a result, in 2005, Seven & I Holdings Co. was formed to become the parent of both, as well as some other members of the IY group.

IY, through IYG Holding Co., a subsidiary owned with SEJ, bought about 70% of bankrupt Southland in 1991. Under Japanese control, the U.S.-based Seven-Eleven chain was transformed so that today the only legacies of Southland are the "7-Eleven" logo and some parts of the accounting system. In 2005 SEJ acquired IY's interest in IYG, giving SEJ a direct and indirect ownership interest in Seven-Eleven of 73%. Then, in September, IYG tendered for the remaining 27% of Seven-Eleven shares.

Chairman and CEO of SEJ, Toshifumi Suzuki, is known as the father of the convenience store industry in Japan. He opened the first store and worked his way to the top of SEJ. In 1992, he became president and CEO of parent IY, and holds those titles at the successor holding company.

SEJ's business operations are explained by the interlinking dynamics of knowledge vision, driving objectives, dialogues, practices, and *ba* and external networks.

Absolute Value and Pursuit of Fundamentals

SEJ's knowledge vision is to predict and respond to evolving customer needs. The absolute value of knowledge vision is captured in the statements "adaptation to change" and "pursuit of fundamentals" in the corporate philosophy, and CEO Suzuki's fundamental question: "What does the customer want?" This enables SEJ to challenge, break, and recreate past practices. Mr. Suzuki's claim that there is no universal franchising management model further indicates that the SEJ business operations are highly context-sensitive. The products and services are geared to meet changing customer demand in various regions and countries.

In the convenience store industry, there is evidence that the best-selling products offer unique features. Imitation, according to Mr. Suzuki, is merely processes of the extending past. He notes that "Our competitors are our customers' needs and wants; not other stores." In fact, past success imposes a paradox of unwanted plenty, which can occur when consumers have difficulty finding what they want even when there is a variety of products available. This may easily lead to a downward spiral, as the wrong products decrease customer loyalty and profits and frequently promote even more frantic imitation. Convenience store chains, according to Mr. Suzuki, are successful only by denying the past and constantly reflecting on the future to find fundamental solutions.

Opportunity Loss

SEJ's driving objective is the "reduction of lost opportunities" through a constant "hypothesis development and testing" spiral. Lost opportunities occur because of the inability to provide the needed products or services at the right place or time. Constant opportunity detection enables SEJ to evolve with customer needs. The most important long-term impact on operations is the realized opportunities in product and service development. Examples range from ¥100 rice balls to banking services. The driving objectives, therefore, explain in part both the high profitability and the steady introduction of innovative products and services over the years. This is because the operational fundamentals have remained the same despite the increasingly harsh retailing environment in Japan.

To realize its vision of adapting to changing customer needs, SEJ has to cut opportunity loss by avoiding situations where a consumer coming to a store does not finding what is wanted and leaves. Unlike inventory cost from overstocking, opportunity loss from unrealized sales is invisible and difficult to grasp absent such a mantra. Instead, it is buried in tacit insights gained through consumer interaction. Rather than follow orders from a manual, employees need to think and act based on their subjective insights. Despite the increased role of information technology in the convenience store industry, SEJ operations are largely based on the power of human insights.

At SEJ, placing orders is a responsibility of every employee at each store, including even high school students working at the store part-time. Instead of constructing a sophisticated centralized ordering system as Wal-Mart Stores, Inc. has done, SEJ delegates responsibility to local employees. This is based on the belief that the people who work at the store know their customers best.

Employees are asked to build a hypothesis about sales of items every time they place an order. For example, to order soft drinks, they consider if there are any special events such as road construction, a local festival, or a baseball game at a nearby school, as well as the weather forecast. Such specific knowledge is available only to someone actually in the community. By incorporating such local knowledge every day, SEJ cuts opportunity loss.

Hypothesis Development

Various venues are established to synthesize tacit knowledge at SEJ. The sharing of tacit knowledge through weekly meetings and visits to stores by operation field counselors (OFCs) enables SEJ to modify business operations to reflect changing reality. The reinforced linkage between the bottom-up and the top-down realities helps find solutions to prevailing problems and prevents being caught off guard by unanticipated environmental occurrences.

Headquarters Meetings

SEJ is the only company in Japan that regularly holds weekly meetings of more than 1,000 people. The most important is the OFC meeting every Tuesday morning at Tokyo headquarters. Here, franchisers, OFCs, and SEJ employees share tacit knowledge to find ways to provide services. CEO Suzuki participates and communicates management policies, marketing research findings, and prevailing management problems. Reinforcing the knowledge vision, Mr. Suzuki addresses the question of "What does the customer want?" at every meeting.

In the afternoon, OFCs assemble by region to map out tactics for executing the strategies. A key part of this exercise is to consider local factors such as weather, road construction, advertising programs, and activities such as sporting events.

They also take into account any local trends in consumer tastes. Tuesday night, the OFCs fly back to their regions. The next morning, they visit their stores to deliver the messages developed at headquarters and help the stores implement the tactics recommended for the week.

Information systems development personnel attend the OFC meetings to discuss practical problems and ways to develop the information system. The former head of the Information Systems Department, Makoto Usui, says his job "was to provide solutions to the problems that arise at the convenience store rather than the development of the system itself." The components in the information system act as a concrete linkage between the subjective shop-floor reality and objective decision-making tools at headquarters. When information systems–related issues arise in the meeting, priority is given to quick problem solving.

Managers meet every Monday. In the morning they review the previous week's performance and in the afternoon they develop strategies. The participants are ready to make presentations about their field of responsibility. While the data show an objectified view of reality, managers seek to anticipate future trends by reflecting their tacit knowledge through context-specific metaphors.

Emphasis is placed on implementation speed. Mr. Suzuki expects managers facing problems to leave the meeting so that they can immediately solve those problems, and to report the actions, as well as the early results of those actions. The conclusions of the meeting are debriefed to OFCs on Tuesday.

These weekly gatherings are costly. SEJ spends about ¥2.4 billion annually on traveling, lodging, and other related costs. However, the importance of these weekly meetings cannot be explained by a simplistic economic rationale. Although some of the shared information could be transferred through information technology, physical interaction enables the sharing of tacit knowledge through face-to-face dialogue in which a dynamic coherence with the environment is created. Failure to understand and evolve with the changing environment invites lost opportunities in terms of service, product quality, and eventually profits. As a consequence, meetings are important sources of both knowledge and profits.

Practices

The company's practices engender reflection by employees on their actions. New employees both in stores and at headquarters are encouraged to think from the consumers' point of view during the uniform training period. Reflection as a part of daily action is encouraged during frequent OFC visits. State-of-the-art information technology systematizes hypothesis creation, creating a dialectic interaction between subjective and objective knowledge. Accurately formed hypotheses reduce lost opportunities, as the customers find the needed products at nearby stores at the right time.

Training

Training helps employees understand the importance of tacit knowledge in hypothesis creation. Franchisee training places emphasis on practical knowledge accumulated on the shop floor. New franchisees are trained at the central training center for a month, after which they go through a two-month on-the-job (OTJ) training period in a regular store. The program encourages them to constantly think from the customers' perspective. Emphasis is also placed on externalization of ideas to find ways to improve service and product quality.

All part-time employees, who are mostly university students and housewives, are trained in practical skills through observation, guidance, and practice at stores. Internal training is considered more important than formal education.

An important part of part-time workers' OTJ training is product ordering through a point-of-sale (POS) information system. Employees are encouraged to place orders by first thinking from the perspective of an average customer, second from that of an average family, and finally from the perspective of close friends. This helps them to see products and services from diverse standpoints. Employees are constantly sensing various events, such as sports events, construction sites, and other environmental signals potentially influencing sales. Store managers are encouraged to let part-timers take on demanding work and create hypotheses of emerging customer needs because, according to CEO Suzuki, "Responsibility makes work enjoyable and increases independent thinking."

To acquire tacit knowledge in customer interaction, the career of all new employees at SEJ starts with extensive OTJ training in Seven-Eleven stores. As part of job rotation, new employees are required to work in a variety of functions for about two years to accumulate experience in dealing directly with customers and managing stores. For this purpose, a small number of stores are owned and operated directly. Employee experience–derived tacit knowledge provides the basis for decision making at all organizational echelons. Some employees later become OFCs, acting as an important knowledge link between headquarters and stores.

One unique instrument of SEJ for accumulating and disseminating tacit knowledge at the shop floor and throughout the organization is *burabura sha-in* (walking-around employees). These young employees work in the Product Planning Department. Their task is to wander around in stores and socialize with customers. This brings in new insights, especially from young customers. Their accumulated knowledge is converted to explicit form in company reports. This method can be considered an efficient way of collecting information.

OFCs

The OFCs give stores advice on planning, hypothesis creation, information systems, and so on. They are middle managers linking headquarters and the front lines through the regionally based zone managers to whom they report. As such, they are part of what is called "middle-up-down" management. That is, OFCs systematize tacit knowledge gained from customers and deliver it to upper organizational echelons. They further internalize visions through interactions with top managers, and take the roles of instructor, coach, mentor, and coordinator to facilitate knowledge creation.

Each OFC is responsible for a number of stores, each of which is visited twice a week for two to three hours. During that time, the OFC shares knowledge about new products and gives practical advice. The close social interaction processes enable OFCs to absorb tacit knowledge about customer preferences in a specific time and context. An OFC who notices an innovative idea at one store can quickly disseminate it to other stores and to zone managers. The zone managers, who can be considered upper-level managers, transfer knowledge to other OFCs, management at headquarters, and so on, through meetings and other face-to-face interactions.

Information System

SEJ has reformed its information system five times. At a cost of ¥60 billion to develop, the current, fifth-generation, system was introduced in 1999. It connects the stores, distribution centers, manufacturers, headquarters, OFCs, and district offices through satellite telecommunications and an integrated digital network. The stores are provided with multimedia information, such as moving and still pictures, audio, text, and numerical data. Employees can check product information and display methods, the company's current television commercials, and weather and events. SEJ provides information about past orders, sales records, sold-out stocks, sales trends, and new products. Moreover, the system enables each store to create a database of sales performance figures.

In hypothesis creation, the system links subjective intuition with accumulated objective knowledge at the shop floor. In the system, employees determine order entry volumes based on a hypothesis the employees have formulated. Hypotheses are developed by embracing environmental knowledge (customer interaction, observations, etc.) and information (sales records, etc.). When placing orders, employees can hypothesize, for example, that consumption of beer and fast food will increase tomorrow due to a local festival. To increase the accuracy of the hypothesis, consumption patterns of previous local festivals can be checked. As the order is placed, it is checked against accumulated sales data to see whether the hypothesis is consistent with previous experience. Product ordering is the most important part of the convenience store business because it is based on embracing environmental tacit knowledge.

The POS data collected include more than just the items purchased and the exact time of purchase. Employees also enter information on the customer, including gender and age. This information, plus data on where the item was displayed and the exact time of the transaction, is combined in a transaction record. These records are collected and analyzed at headquarters three times a day in a process that takes roughly 20 minutes. Given the number of customer visits to stores, SEJ analyzed about 9.8 million POS transactions daily in 2003. The detailed information on how many goods were sold to what kind of customers is accumulated and used in future product development. The data warehouse accumulates more than one year's worth of sales data per item and supports refined objective analysis for sales forecasting.

In addition to POS data, SEJ collects information on trends (consumer behavior, lifestyles and habits, business trends, etc.), market movements (corporate strategies, product life cycles, etc.), regional differences (population changes, school events, etc.), and weather forecasts.

An interesting detail is the weather information system. Five times each day, reports arrive electronically from hundreds of weather centers, each covering a radius of 20 kilometers. This is beneficial because temperatures between stores 40 kilometers apart can vary by as much as 5 degrees Celsius.

SEJ uses sales trends in deciding whether to keep or drop an item. Typically, a new product reaches its sales peak within a week or two and begins to decline several weeks later. When per store sales drop to a certain level, the product is deleted from the recommended list. The life of most products has shrunk over time. This means new products are being introduced and older products are being dropped at a faster rate. Of the 3,000 SKUs carried by each store, about half are replaced every year.

The data can be used to adjust store layout several times a day. For example, a store may detect differences in the type of ice cream sold at different times. Using the data and tacit intuition, employees can arrange the ice cream display to highlight items favored for the time of day.

Analysis of several years of data by Noriyuki Ikeda, head of dairy products, found that yogurt sales rise when influenza is common. During the next influenza season, stores were alerted to this and stocked accordingly. This led to yogurt sales twice the usual level, showing the opportunity gain of anticipating customer needs.

Ba and External Networks

SEJ cooperates with various external partners to introduce new products and services. The knowledge combination in team-merchandizing projects enables the introduction of original products, and stable relationships with suppliers and other external partners are essential for the incremental improvements. These types of collaboration, based on open knowledge exchange and combination, provide benefits to all involved parties.

Distribution System

The stores are connected by an online information system to almost 300 distribution centers nationwide, as well as to almost 300 plants that make short-lived items such as lunch boxes and rice balls. These short-life items are delivered three times a day. Other items, including frozen products, are delivered three to seven times per week. Separate distribution centers deliver books and magazines every day.

The core of distribution improvement is frequent human interaction. To increase efficiency, SEJ holds regular meetings with the heads of combined distribution centers. (These centers bring products together in a single location and sort them for individual stores.) Moreover, distribution officers from the headquarters pay regular visits to the centers to address problems. This knowledge sharing enables them to identify areas for improvement at the centers and in the information system.

The information system enables quick data processing. For example, orders sent by 10 am for delivery after 4 pm can be processed electronically in less than seven minutes. Because of rapid delivery times, SEJ eliminated preservatives in most fast food items in 2002. Moreover, there is no need to carry large inventories and little loss due to excess production.

Team Merchandizing

SEJ cooperates with vendors and manufacturers through team merchandizing to create and introduce original products. External collaboration is important, as original products constitute an important share of total sales. (Net sales of original products accounted for about half of total sales in 2003.) They also make a substantial contribution in the gross profit margin, as original items typically have higher margins than regular products.

The most important vehicle of external cooperation with food suppliers is Nihon Delica Foods (NDF), established in 1979. NDF, in which 88 manufacturers are involved, works on merchandise development, quality control, joint purchase, and the like.

Team merchandizing is a systematized process, starting with determining market needs and deciding what type of product to introduce. Market need is based on POS data, surveys, and tacit knowledge from customer interface. The constant interplay of subjective and objective knowledge makes it possible to break conventional assumptions. For example, interpretation of POS data revealed that premium ice cream sells well all year. SEJ was also the first to develop oven-fresh bread, exploiting a gap between consumer preferences and the products supplied by national-brand bread makers.

SEJ approaches manufacturers with product ideas and seeks feasibility and production cost feedback. Value is the most important way to attract customers, so manufacturers emphasize product quality. To develop its premium ice cream, SEJ approached five major manufacturers. Morinaga Milk, Morinaga, and Akagi Milk decided to jointly develop the product. The ice cream was a success, selling substantially more than existing products. In developing the oven-fresh bread, SEJ collaborated with food makers such as Ajinomoto Co., Inc., Ito-chu Corporation, and local bakeries. The bread helped SEJ differentiate itself from competitors.

Team merchandizing is based on open knowledge sharing. SEJ starts by sharing POS data to create an understanding of the target customers for the new product. Facilitated by a shared vision and complementary knowledge, the most intense knowledge sharing occurs at meetings in which manufacturers improve products by sharing samples, recipes, and other related know-how. Development requires several meetings before a product is ready for final approval. For example, it took 18 months to develop the right taste for the fried rice.

Production starts after final approval at the officers' meeting. SEJ's goal is to systematize the process by creating "dream teams." For example, a noodle project tied five well-known noodle manufacturers with three soup makers, five condiment makers, two package makers, and six noodle restaurants.

Knowledge Alliances

SEJ diversifies its services with various joint arrangements and affiliated companies. This has been facilitated by the information system, regulatory changes, changing consumer preferences, and a wide external network.

SEJ has been committed to electronic commerce. In 2000 it established a virtual shopping mall called 7dream.com in cooperation with several other large companies, including NEC, Nomura Research Institute, and Sony. Over 100,000 items are offered in six categories: music, travel and leisure, general merchandise, automotive products, photographs, and Internet products. The concept is simple: the order is made on the Web site, and then delivered directly or to a Seven-Eleven store where it can be picked up.

Regulatory changes and the relative insensitivity of Japanese banks to customer needs motivated SEJ to start a bank in 2001. Initially called IY Bank, the name changed to Seven Bank in October 2005. The bank operates solely through automatic teller machines (ATMs) located in its stores. It has no other street presence. Most stores operate 24 hours a day, and SEJ's ATMs were among the first to allow around-the-clock banking. In contrast, the ATMs of most Japanese banks can be used only until 8 pm. In order to provide a wide range of financial services, the bank has links with 49 other financial institutions. In April 2005 more than 10,098 ATMs had been installed in 25 prefectures.

New services are introduced based on a systematic search to identify market needs through embracing customer tacit knowledge, monitoring regulatory changes, and contacting external partners for cooperation. The introduced services are related to, or seek to complement, existing competencies. As Kenichi Yamamoto from SEJ's Information Department notes, "These services fill a gap in our over-the-counter services." SEJ innovations have changed customer preferences.

Foreign Operations

As the Japanese retail market matured, SEJ began expanding internationally. Including the foreign network of its U.S.-based Seven-Eleven subsidiary, the chain operates in 18 countries and territories.[1]

The biggest growth potential has been identified as China. SEJ entered China in January 2002 in a joint venture with Beijing ShouLian (Capital Allied) Commercial Group Co., Ltd. and China National Sugar & Alcohol Group Corp. The Seven-Eleven opened on Dongzhimen Street in Beijing's Dongchen district in April 2004 was the first Chinese-foreign joint venture convenience store in China. The store is 187 square meters, which is quite a bit larger than the average Japanese store—though still somewhat smaller than stores in the United States.

SEJ opened 60 outlets in 2004 and plans to open 300 in Guangzhou and 500 in Beijing by 2009. Operations are expected to spread to Shanghai in 2006. At the moment, SEJ has only directly managed stores, but seeks to open franchising stores in the near future.

Chinese operations indicate how SEJ seeks to replicate part of its retail know-how, including being sensitive to local tastes. For example, SEJ has done considerable effort to adapt group-merchandizing techniques used in Japan to China's operation environment. SEJ is looking at specific ways of developing high-quality connections between stores, delivery units, and manufacturers.

Employee training and management practices are also being transferred from Japan. For example, empowerment of responsibilities has guaranteed high commitment among local employees. Emphasis in the training is on using external knowledge through social interaction with customers. SEJ is committed to providing products and services that suit local customer needs and wants. Thus, Beijing stores have in-store cooking facilities while Japanese stores do not.

While it is too early to make any concrete assumptions about SEJ's operations in China, using contextual local tacit knowledge to create services and goods that fit with local tastes has proven to be highly successful. Based on the company, Chinese customers have responded favorably to stores, with fast-food offerings proving particularly popular.

Primary Components of SEJ's Success

The goal of SEJ is to be flexible with regard to change, as well as committed to its fundamental principle of responding to rapidly changing consumer needs. Headquarters and affiliated stores share the belief that competition is not with the other companies or stores, but with the consumer and consumer needs and wants. The components facilitating this process are shown in Figure 2.2.

---

1. As of February 2005, there were 27,727 stores in the United States, Taiwan, China, Thailand, the Republic of Korea, China, Mexico, Canada, Malaysia, Australia, Singapore, the Philippines, Norway, Sweden, Turkey, Denmark, Puerto Rico, Guam, and Japan. Not all of these are Seven-Elevens. Other banners include Christy's Markets, High's Dairy Store, and Quick Marts.

Figure 2.2.   *Knowledge-Creating Components of SEJ*

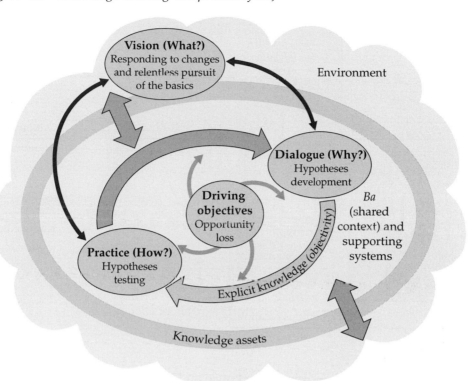

The components separate SEJ from retail companies that tend to focus on inventory reduction and simplistic part-time employee roles. Instead of following daily routines, all employees at SEJ are encouraged to utilize their context-specific tacit knowledge and to have a future- and customer-oriented mindset. The creative combination of contextual tacit knowledge and information technology as a competitive advantage is emphasized in employee training, employee interaction, meetings, and the like.

Opportunity losses are minimized through knowledge creation. To accumulate tacit knowledge, store staff is asked by OFCs to pay attention to local community activities. Employees externalized the accumulated knowledge, for example, through hypothetical dialogues at store back offices. Weekly OFC meetings and team merchandizing are other examples of activities through which knowledge is externalized. The externalized knowledge is combined through the use of information technology, such as graphic-order terminals. The data are processed several times a day. SEJ helps employees internalize knowledge by teaching hypothesis creation and verification through OTJ training.

The combination of tacit and explicit knowledge makes SEJ an existential company. This was apparent in a 2004 advertising campaign, which asked "What does the number 7 mean to you?" The question was formulated by CEO Suzuki to encourage both customers and employees to reflect on the products and services of their neighborhood Seven-Eleven.

While the visionary leadership of CEO Suzuki has contributed to the company's success, the business model and internalization of knowledge among top managers can be reasonably expected to keep SEJ at the top of Japanese convenience store operations even as leadership changes.

Figure 2.3. *Supporting* Ba *at SEJ*

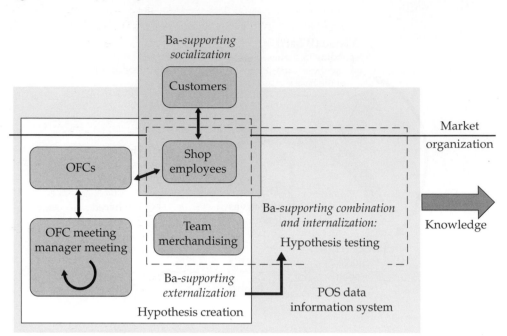

Knowledge creation is dynamic and open and includes various interconnected actors, such as customers and suppliers, within and beyond organizational boundaries. Various *ba*s support hypothesis creation at all parts of the convenience store chain (Figure 2.3).

Hypotheses are created by shop employees in customer interaction, by OFCs in weekly meetings and in interacting with employees in shops, and by the participants of team-merchandizing programs in interacting with SEJ employees and other manufacturers. Although some of these practices can be copied by other companies, tacit knowledge embedded into the system is not transferable.

People in these linked *ba*s utilize tacit knowledge through the future-oriented reflection of present activities, which enables utilizing past experiences efficiently. That is, the desire to fulfill future consumer needs opens new meanings to past purchase patterns. This ontology gives rise to the detection of opportunities leading to an endless repetition of hypothesizing, execution, and evaluation at SEJ. The knowledge creation process is extended to interactions with external partners.

SEJ's practices have been introduced successfully outside Japan through social interaction. In most cases, task forces are sent to start operations and to transfer tacit knowledge to local employees. For example, in China local employees have been taught merchandizing assortment, service quality, customer interaction, and product ordering.

While other convenience store chains, such as Lawson and Familymart, have imitated some SEJ practices, they have been unable to catch up with SEJ. The distinctive ability of SEJ is to constantly transcend its practices through self-knowledge and collective knowledge creation. As a consequence, SEJ has been able to link its products and services to evolving customer needs and wants better than its rivals.

Conclusion

This chapter shows that knowledge creation takes place through a dialectic interaction between agents and environment, and tacit and explicit knowledge. Knowledge visions, driving objectives, dialogues, practices, and *ba* are the reinforcing components. Instead of viewing firms detached from the environment, tacit knowledge in action links people and firms with their surrounding reality. Knowledge is frequently created through networked linkages, as knowledge sharing among diverse sets of entities speeds the knowledge creation processes. This allows the conceptualization of firms as networked entities and as social exchange systems with distinctive rules, trust, and knowledge transfer and creation practices.

SEJ illustrates the knowledge creation process. The company dynamically interlocks dialogue and practice with opportunity loss as the driving objective. Moreover, mutual environmental interactions take place at different phases between practice and dialogue, such as incorporating tacit knowledge embedded in the environment through practice (integration of subject and object) and transcending this tacit knowledge by a thorough conceptualization of dialogue (separation of subject and object). The ontology of SEJ is future orientation because emerging customer needs drive operations. The focus on customer interface enables employees to utilize past experiences in the present reality. The epistemology of SEJ takes place through the objectification of subjective insights by hypothesis testing.

Sharing and systematizing practices has allowed SEJ to develop hard-to-imitate knowledge assets. Knowledge assets help make SEJ the most innovative convenience store chain, and are one of the important components of SEJ's micro practices in strategizing. Many convenience stores in Japan and overseas seek to follow SEJ's model. However, they have not been able to compete with SEJ's relentless pursuit of meeting constantly evolving customer needs and wants.

The case study in this chapter is a descriptive and context-specific illustration of how one successful convenience store chain has innovated over time in co-evolution with its environment. The purpose is not to provide a normative model of evolutionary change, as predicting innovative events in organizations is seldom possible. It can, though, be asserted that all companies create knowledge through dialectic identification, processing, and developing processes toward more inclusive totalities. It can be further assumed that knowledge-creating action is founded on the mechanisms of knowledge vision, dialogues, and practices, as well as on the knowledge creation process.

References

Collins, Jim. 2001. *Good to Great: Why Some Companies Make the Leap . . . and Others Don't.* New York: Harper Business.

Depraz, N., Varela, F., and Vermersch, P. 2003. *On Becoming Aware: A Pragmatic of Experiencing.* Amsterdam: John Bejamins.

Heidegger, Martin. 1962. *Being and Time.* New York: Harper & Row.

Husserl, Edmund. 1931. *Ideas: General Introduction to Pure Phenomenology.* WRB translation. New York: Macmillan.

Lawson, Tony. 1997. *Economics and Reality.* New York: Routledge.

Nelson, Richard, and Sidney Winter. 1982. *An Evolutionary Theory of Economic Change.* Cambridge, MA: Harvard University Press.

Nishida, Kitaro. 1990. *An Inquiry into the Good.* New Haven: Yale University Press. Original work published in 1921.

Nonaka, Ikujiro. 1991. "The Knowledge Creating-Company." *Harvard Business Review* 79 (1): 96–104.

Nonaka, Ikujiro. 1994. "A Dynamic Theory of Organizational Knowledge Creation." *Organizational Science* 5 (1): 14–37.

Nonaka, Ikujiro, and Noburu Konno. 1998. "The Concept of 'Ba': Building a Foundation for Knowledge Creation." *California Management Review* 40 (3): 40–55.

Nonaka, Ikujiro, and Hirotaka Takeuchi. 1995. *The Knowledge-Creating Company: How Japanese Companies Create the Dynamics of Innovation.* New York: Oxford University Press.

Nonaka, Ikujiro, Vesa Peltokorpi, and D. Senoo. (forthcoming). "Knowledge Creation in Japanese Convenience Store Chain: The Case of Seven-Eleven Japan." In J. R. Bryson and P. W. Daniels, editors, *The Service Industries Handbook.* Cheltenham: Edward Elgar.

Nonaka, Ikujiro, Vesa Peltokorpi, and Hisao Tomae. 2005. "Strategic Knowledge Creation: The Case of Hamamatsu Photonics." *International Journal of Technology Management* 30 (3/4): 248–64.

Nonaka, Ikujiro, and Ryoko Toyama. 2002. "A Firm as a Dialectical Being: Towards a Dynamic Theory of a Firm." *Industrial and Corporate Change* 11 (5): 995–1009.

Nonaka, Ikujiro, and Ryoko Toyama. 2003. "The Knowledge-Creating Theory Revisited: Knowledge Creation as a Synthesizing Process." *Knowledge Management Research & Practice* 1 (1): 2–10.

Polanyi, Michael. 1952. *Personal Knowledge.* Chicago: The University of Chicago Press.

Shön, Donald A. 1983. *The Reflective Practitioner.* New York: Basic Books.

Takeuchi, Hirotaka, and Ikujiro Nonaka, editors. 2004. *Hitotsubashi on Knowledge Management.* Singapore: Wiley.

3

Learning and the Self-Renewing, Network Organization: Toyota and Lexus Dealers

Emi Osono

One source of competitiveness in Japanese companies that has been the subject of intensive study is the stable relationship between manufacturers and suppliers. This chapter analyzes such relationships in terms of the social capital of a network organization. Social capital is what enables an organization to learn to improve, to adapt to environmental changes, and to change themselves. A network organization is a group of companies with a relatively stable membership and close working relationships between the constituents.

Many studies have attributed the competitiveness of Japanese automobile manufacturers such as Toyota and Honda to the relationships they have with their suppliers. The focus here is on carmakers and dealers (retailers). This contrasts with the usual focus on automobile parts suppliers (Box 3.1).

The chapter is organized as follows. First, the concepts of network organizations, social capital, and knowledge management are presented. Next, an overview is provided of Lexus and its dealers. With this context, Toyota and Lexus dealers are analyzed as a network organization. Creating Toyota's social capital is then taken up, with sections on how Toyota relates to the structural, relational, and cognitive dimensions of social capital.

The questions of how a network organization can adapt to environmental changes and whether Lexus' success in network-building can be transplanted are also addressed.

Network Organizations

Network organizations are groups of companies with relatively stable memberships and close working relationships between the constituents. In terms of institutional form, they are between markets and vertically integrated organizations. Indeed, the advantage of a network organization is the fact that it can enjoy the strengths of both the market and a vertically integrated organization. In other words, it can both maintain the economic motivation to maximize the local return that markets provide participants, as well as exert the kind of effective coordination and control mechanism an organization has over its units. However, this is not easy to realize. With poor design and management, a network organization might end up with shortages of profit, coordination, and control.

Typically, network organizations are found in industries that have integral product architecture, such as automobiles and aircraft. Thus, the Japanese automobile industry, involving parts suppliers and final assemblers, is the archetypal example. The organizational form is applicable and competitive in other geographic areas, as well as

> **Box 3.1.**   *Auto Parts Suppliers*
>
> Within an automobile manufacturing network organization, parts suppliers can special-ize in particular parts and deepen their knowledge of that field. They are able to con-duct continuous improvement based on both the motivation provided by competition with other, and similar suppliers in charge of the same parts, as well as expected rewards. At the same time, they are internalizing production know-how, such as the Toyota Production System, which continues to evolve while being applied to different suppliers. This allows the assemblers to focus on developing the product concept and system designs, high-value-added parts such as engines and bodies, and strategic issues such as product planning, international strategy, and long-term issues such as alterna-tive power sources.

in non-Japanese companies. It has been applied outside of Japan by Japanese car-makers, and they have been able to successfully add non-Japanese suppliers.

The concepts are applicable in other industrial settings. An example is retailers engaged in "team merchandising" with brand-name manufacturers in order to have their retail knowledge reflected in product development while providing shelf space to the manufacturers.

Even in the personal computer and server industries, where products are based on modular architecture and require less coordination among suppliers and assem-blers, Dell Inc. has developed a stable learning relationship with its suppliers in order to improve inventory and quality management as a group (Dyer and Hatch 2004). And, in other industries where technologies are complex and often rapidly changing, many companies have established relatively stable relationships with other companies that possess technological capabilities they lack.

Emergence of the Concept

In the latter half of the 1990s, some academics began to speak of organizations as deposits of knowledge: creating, obtaining, combining, improving, and storing it (Nonaka and Takeuchi 1995; Nahapiet and Ghoshal 1998; Ghoshal et al. 1999).

These studies provided not only an alternative to transaction cost theory's explanation regarding why and when organizations are needed, but also appraised the unique features of organizations.

Transaction cost theory argues that organizations are needed to overcome trans-action costs, such as searching for mutually agreeable conditions and monitoring opportunistic behaviors, and assumes market mechanisms are ideal. However, when the knowledge creation process is understood as sharing tacit knowledge, converting tacit to explicit knowledge, combining explicit knowledge, and chang-ing explicit to tacit knowledge by internalizing it (Nonaka and Takeuchi 1995), mar-ket mechanisms look less ideal. Instead, it becomes clear that it is necessary to share the experience, understand others' context in order to see their point of view, and reduce the risk of sharing information or knowledge.

Thus, from a knowledge management perspective, historically organizations typically have been better off when they develop internal structures and proce-dures than when they rely solely on markets to provide needed knowledge. However, in many industries it has become difficult to do everything within an organization: network organizations are a possible solution to this problem.

Therefore, in this chapter, network organizations are studied from a knowledge management perspective in order to illustrate how they can be good environments for learning and self-renewing. To achieve this goal, a framework based on the social capital theory developed by Nahapiet and Ghoshal (1998) is applied to the case of Lexus, Toyota's luxury car business. The focus is on the relationship between Toyota and Lexus dealers in the United States.

Social Capital and Knowledge Management

Various organizational factors promote knowledge sharing and creation. Scholars of organizational learning from an operation management background, Garvin (1993) for example, have identified several factors: systemic problem solving; experimentation; learning from past experiences (including failures) using postproject reviews and developing knowledge databases; learning from others (including customers and, by benchmarking, competitors); and transferring knowledge using site visits, personnel rotation, standardization, and training.

Nonaka and Takeuchi (1995) identified five: intention to give direction to uncertain innovation processes; autonomy; fluctuation and creative chaos that bring change to the status quo; redundancy, in the sense of the overlapping information and roles that make effective communication possible; and requisite variety (or at least the same degree of variety within the organization as is present in the environment). Vision—"what does a company exist for?"—was subsequently added by Nonaka. (See chapter 2 in volume 2, by Nonaka.)

Innovation management scholars consider other factors for knowledge creation. These include experimentation, psychological safety for failures, linkage among diversified knowledge that sometimes goes beyond organizational boundaries, champions and coaches who protect innovations from the operational routines of established organizations and organizational politics, well-coordinated cross-functional teams (heavyweight teams), and organizational motivation for innovation, among others.

All the organizational factors mentioned are important for knowledge sharing and creation. However, for the interorganizational situations this chapter addresses—that is, where independent economic entities have their own identity, assets, goals, stakeholders, and business models—some additional, fundamental factors should also be addressed. These include: What motivates participants of the network organization to share their knowledge? How does accessibility of other participants' knowledge affect learning and knowledge creation? What makes communication among diversified perspectives and creation of new knowledge possible?

These are addressed here using the framework developed by Nahapiet and Ghoshal (1998), which is based on the theory of social capital. Social capital facilitates the development of intellectual capital by affecting conditions such as access to parties with knowledge, anticipation of value, motivation to exchange or combine knowledge, and combination capability, which are necessary for exchange and combination to occur. This is illustrated in Figure 3.1.

The Characteristics of Social Capital

To understand the characteristics of social capital, it can be analyzed from three dimensions: structural, relational, and cognitive. Later, these are applied specifically to Toyota and the dealers.

Figure 3.1.   *Social Capital and Knowledge Creation*

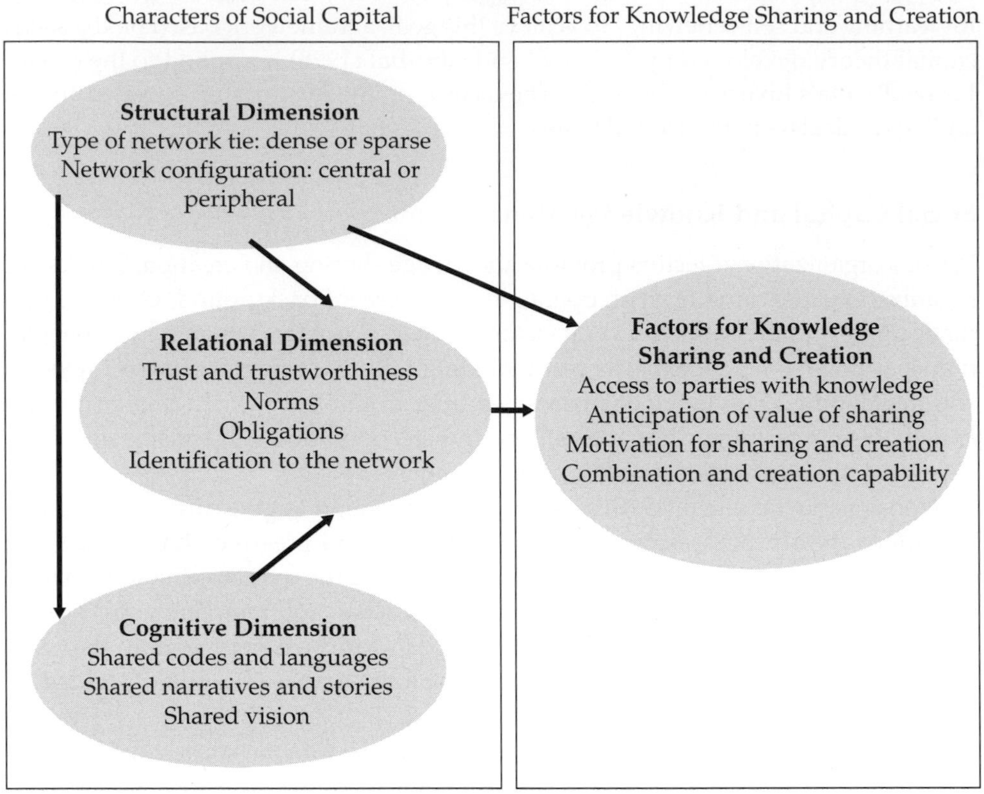

Characters of Social Capital   Factors for Knowledge Sharing and Creation

Structural Dimension
Type of network tie: dense or sparse
Network configuration: central or
peripheral

Relational Dimension
Trust and trustworthiness
Norms
Obligations
Identification to the network

**Factors for Knowledge
Sharing and Creation**
Access to parties with knowledge
Anticipation of value of sharing
Motivation for sharing and creation
Combination and creation capability

Cognitive Dimension
Shared codes and languages
Shared narratives and stories
Shared vision

Source: Adopted from Nahapiet & Ghoshal (1998) and Tsai & Ghoshal (1998).

Structural Dimension

The structural dimension of social capital refers to the types of network ties (sparse or dense) and the participants' positions in the network configuration (central or peripheral).

A dense network has redundant contacts, hence more of the same information is shared among participants and they share information more efficiently. A sparse network has more diversified information. Best practices and innovations are shared more rapidly and broadly in dense networks than in sparse networks, hence there is continuous improvement of system performance. Sparse networks provide a favorable environment for radical innovation, which requires diversified knowledge to be integrated.

Those participants positioned at the center of the network have access to more information, while those at the periphery have less. The former are better positioned to learn from other participants and share their own knowledge with others, while the latter are sometimes better positioned to innovate, as they face different environments and are less constrained by group norms. Hence, "innovations happen on the periphery."

Moreover, innovative organizations have "gatekeepers" who have more access to external information and translate it to internal participants so that they can understand external information in their context and be part of innovation initiatives. In other words, incremental innovations or improvements are likely to be started by those at the center, while radical innovations are likely to be started by those at the periphery. Thus, a network organization that is involved in both incremental and radical innovation needs to have core participants at the center of the network, as well as peripheral participants.

Relational Dimension

The relational dimension refers to the relationship of interactions. Examples are trust, shared norms, obligations, and identifications, which can function as governance mechanisms. Strength in this dimension decreases the risk of sharing information by lowering the possibility of other participants' opportunistic behavior, and improves the anticipated value of knowledge sharing. Trust allows participants to admit shortcomings and acknowledge areas needing improvement, which is necessary for improvement and learning from others to take place.

Norms such as openness to criticism, tolerance of failure, and willingness to value diversity encourage the experimentation necessary for improvement and innovation, and help a network organization avoid conformity and group-think.

Cognitive Dimension

The cognitive dimension refers to shared codes and languages, and shared narratives such as myths, stories, and metaphors. These provide the shared context and overlapping knowledge that makes meaningful communication and knowledge sharing possible. Stories can convey tacit nuances and enable common interpretations of shared reality. Shared visions and ideals inspire the participants to improve and direct interactions toward the same goal.

Lexus and Lexus Dealers

Toyota Motor Corporation and Lexus dealers are an example of best practices in a number of areas. As such, they are not a typical case study. The case portrays a network organization that enjoys both the benefits of market mechanisms and organization form. That is, each participating organization pursues its own benefits, demonstrating entrepreneurship and creativity while sharing knowledge and learning from each other, and achieving competitiveness as a whole by maintaining a coherent system. The Lexus network organization has been successful because it continuously improves its operations with an attitude of "relentless pursuit of perfection," and incrementally adapts to market changes. At the same time, it maintains a coherent system as a whole, and has not changed its business model.

Lexus was introduced in the United States in 1989, and has been very successful in the ensuing years. It obtained top market share in the U.S. luxury car segment by surpassing Mercedes Benz in 2000. The cars have repeatedly ranked at the top in initial vehicle quality, as well as quality after three years, and the used car market has placed a relatively high resale value on them.

Lexus has been very profitable for both Toyota and Lexus dealers. The company has not disclosed the total investment for the model's launch, but each dealer invested between $3 million and $5 million to erect an independent dealership building with standardized exteriors and interiors, and to install an information technology system. The satellite communication system linking the IT systems was paid for by Toyota and is estimated to have cost something over $3 million.

No other new brand has established itself so quickly and successfully as Lexus did in the United States. Toyota did this by differentiating the Lexus from other luxury brands in terms of both the vehicles and the dealer experience.

The vehicles are often described as having "understated" design, even as competing brands have pushed the limits of design and engine power. But even more important, Lexus displays craftsmanship, and the quality lasts over time. Thus, they are described as "tomb-quiet," the result of substantially reducing the noise and vibration caused by the engine, air flow, and the road. This reflects both design and precision in processing parts and assembly. Craftsmanship extends to smaller details: all wood in the interior of a vehicle comes from the same tree so that the grain matches, even on lower-priced models. Materials are chosen to minimize loss of color and wear even after 10 years.

The Lexus covenant asks dealers to treat customers as though they are guests in their homes. To support this, sales and service personnel are on salary rather than the more common industry practice, which is heavily skewed toward commissions. There is generally no price negotiation.

Dealers are continually seeking ways to improve service, and they share best practices. Some dealers even offer meal coupons for customers waiting to have their cars serviced. The company maintains files on each car sold in order to provide efficient service. The result is high customer satisfaction with the sales and service experience at Lexus dealerships. Surveys indicate that Lexus customers are among the most satisfied in the luxury segment.

Toyota and Lexus Dealers as a Network Organization

U.S. automobile dealers are not owned by automobile companies. Dealers selling the same brand compete with each other, and the better ones survive. The opposite is vertical integration. In Germany, by owning dealers, Peugeot has been able to enjoy strict control of the sales and service process, and obtain retail information directly. This has been very beneficial to Peugeot as a weak player that experienced difficulties attracting capable dealers in the German market.

Toyota employs a third form in most countries. This is a network organization of independently owned dealerships. (In Japan, prior to the 2005 launch of the Lexus in Japan, Toyota owned 8% of its sales outlets. In comparison, Honda owns 30% of its dealerships.) Toyota believes this leads to more entrepreneurial and more customer-centric dealerships, rather than product- or factory-centric ones.

The network organization consisting of Toyota Motor Sales (TMS, Toyota's U.S. sales subsidiary) and Lexus dealers has four key characteristics: stable membership, relatively small number of participants, shared norms and values, and a multi-layered communication network.

Lexus dealers and Toyota have an intensive communication network of multiple layers that exchange tacit knowledge such as values, norms, know-how, insights, and concerns. This is the key element in the cognitive dimension and, as such, is taken up later in a discussion of specific Toyota practices.

Few Long-Term Dealers

Toyota intentionally limits the number of Lexus dealers and consequently has far fewer than its competitors. Lexus started in 1989 with 81 and a long-term goal of just 200. At that time, Mercedes-Benz and BMW each had more than 400 dealers, and Cadillac and Lincoln each had more than 1,600. In September 2005, Lexus had only 182 dealers, operating 214 showrooms (each of which had service and parts departments). As discussed later, by limiting the number of dealers, the company has more opportunities to have face-to-face communication with dealer management and dealer associates. (In Japan, where Toyota has more than 40% of the market, it has more sales outlets than its competitors, but the number of companies owning dealerships is small. This allows Toyota to maintain better communication and a stronger dealer body, thanks to economies of scale.)

Dealerships have been sold, typically as part of the owners' succession plans. However, in over 15 years, only once has Lexus not renewed a dealer contract for nonperformance of the franchise agreement. Rather than terminating poor performers, the company tries to educate and improve dealers with less satisfactory performances. Stable membership is necessary for learning and knowledge creation among the participants, because time is a key element in building and sharing tacit knowledge, developing relationships among participants, and identifying with the group.

Shared Norms and Values

With shared norms and values, Lexus Division members and dealers identify with Lexus and differentiate themselves from the rest of the Toyota operation. When Lexus was being created, establishing a clear identity and declaring a commitment to dealers, headquarters, customers, and reporters was necessary because many people, even some potential dealers, were skeptical as to whether Toyota could make luxury cars, let alone change the market perception, attract customers, and grow large enough to sustain the new franchise. To articulate the norms and values unique to Lexus, the founding members of the Lexus team in the United States drafted the "Lexus Covenant." The company asked all of the associates in the division, and all the dealer employees who had completed the Lexus educational programs, to sign the Lexus Covenant (Box 3.2).

Commitment to the covenant was demonstrated when Toyota had to recall the first Lexus at the end of 1989, just months after the initial launch and after heavy promotion of Lexus quality. Problems in the LS400 included a tail-lamp case that overheated and deformed, a cruise control that would not turn off, and a battery that died. Only one case of each failure occurred, and no accidents or injuries were involved. Some Toyota managers thought the problem did not warrant a recall because U.S. law requires recalls for parts replacement only if safety issues are involved. By organizing a recall, Lexus was facing the risk of invalidating its marketing message of "built by 1,400 perfectionists" and its tagline, "relentless pursuit of perfection."

The recall, which involved about 8,000 cars, was smooth and quick, which symbolized a commitment to the finest quality of service, as promised by the covenant. TMS planned for completion of the repairs in 20 days, ending before Christmas. Some managers considered this unrealistic: the parts that caused the problems were

---

Box 3.2.   The Lexus Covenant

Lexus will enter the most competitive,
prestigious automobile race in the world.
Over 50 years of Toyota automotive experience
has culminated in the creation of Lexus cars.
They will be the finest cars ever built.

Lexus will win the race because:
Lexus will do it right from the start.
Lexus will have the finest
dealer network in the industry.
Lexus will treat each customer
as we would a guest in our home.

If you think you can't, you won't . . .
If you think you can, you will!
We can, we will.

---

made only for Lexus, and suppliers would have to increase production quickly. Moreover, dealer service personnel had to be trained. Nonetheless, many dealers cleared the target early. As a comparison, when the Toyota Division had a recall in 1984, involving some 91,000 cars in the United States and Canada, parts replacement took a whole year.

A general manager of a Lexus dealership noted: "TMS sent Lexus parts the day the recall was announced. The same day, they sent service personnel to teach us how to do the repairs. I had been in the car retail business with multiple carmakers for 15 years but had never seen such an efficient operation" (*Automotive News*, December 11, 1989).

This demonstrated Toyota's commitment to Lexus values and promoted Lexus dealer understanding and belief in it. At a dealer meeting in March 1990, the first message from the dealer association chair was: "Thank you for the recall." This was followed by his observation of improved dealer reputations, greater solidarity inside the dealer organizations, and dissemination of processes within Lexus servicing, among others. After the recall, many dealers began to start each workday by reciting the Lexus Covenant. The recall story has become a legend among Lexus associates and dealers.

Lexus dealer commitment to their shared norms and values was also exhibited when Lexus business experienced hard times in the mid-1990s due to appreciation of the yen against the dollar. The cars were imported from Japan in those days, making them more expensive. The increased prices came at a time when the current models were getting somewhat stale compared to competitors. Some dealers began offering cash incentives and emphasizing discounts. However, in a meeting with the Lexus Division, the majority of dealers expressed opposition to incentives (especially cash incentives). They felt the practice contradicted the Lexus Division's message of focusing on customer satisfaction and quality. The dealers encouraged the Lexus Division to "return to the basics."

Another value shared among Lexus dealers and Toyota is Toyota's belief that, unless dealers make a profit, Toyota cannot make its own business successful, because dealers will not invest in the people and facilities to continuously improve. This value is expressed in a Toyota slogan carried over to Lexus: "Customer first, dealer second, and factory last." TMS associates often use this expression when making decisions and explaining their behavior.

When other carmakers began direct sales on the Internet, Toyota was very slow to follow. When it finally did, it was with such models as the first-generation Prius, where demand was expected to be limited and carrying inventory was not economical for some dealers. The company uses the Internet most extensively with Scion, but has limited the Internet's function to providing information, configuring cars, and costing, which supports the dealer sales process rather than impinging on it. Scion is Toyota's low-end, or entry-level, line. It targets trendsetters in Generation Y, those born between 1980 and 1994. Based on cars sold in Japan, it was introduced in the United States in 2003.

The Structural Dimension

In terms of types of network ties, the network organization of Toyota and Lexus dealers is very dense. Multiple layers of communication help them share the same values, policies, attitudes, and best practices. At the center of this dense network is Lexus Division, which is positioned to have access to most of the information. In this way, Toyota is able to gather market information and best practices among dealers so that it can develop better product and marketing plans. In other words, by obtaining significant local knowledge, Toyota can be better at system-level knowledge creation. In addition, Toyota can provide consultation and coaching to the dealers, if requested, by functioning as a knowledge depository.

Dealers, on the other hand, face various local realities such as customers, competitors, and local market conditions such as the local economy and local regulations. These sometimes lead to new ideas and practices. Dealers, positioned at the company's periphery, can be a source of innovation.

For the innovations to become the capabilities of other dealers, it is necessary that Toyota know what is going on. This is so it can make sense of useful emerging innovations, and help dealers develop them into standard practices, even changing Toyota itself if necessary. Therefore, Toyota's position at the center of the network matters.

The foundation of the network is visits to dealers by managers from area offices and the Lexus Division. The managers observe and discuss operations, as well as learn from the dealers and provide advice when necessary. The visits, and the various meetings with groups of dealers, enable direct communication with dealers and position Toyota at the center.

There are four area offices, each responsible for 45 or so dealers. Field managers, who are responsible for 5 to 10 dealers, engage in daily communication with dealer managers and staff in charge of sales, service, and finance so that important information can be shared. These contacts are by phone and through regular visits to dealers. The information obtained is reported at monthly area manager meetings and communicated to the Lexus Division of TMS in California. This is one of the primary ways in which best practices and creative customer services are gathered and shared among Lexus managers.

Sales and service managers from the Lexus Division of TMS in California also make frequent visits to dealers. This reflects the attitude and way of doing business shared by all Toyota divisions. It is called *"genchi genbutsu."* (This translates as "go see the actual article at the scene." It is similar to "management by walking around," but with more emphasis on *understanding* on the part of the managers as part of their conscious problem-finding and problem-solving process.) In addition, the chief operating officer of TMS meets with dealership executives, as well as with the personnel in charge of parts, service, and car washing. The resulting notes are passed on to the relevant divisions. This is very unusual behavior for a carmaker in the United States. Even for Japanese carmakers, it was not common practice for representatives of the headquarters divisions or U.S. sales subsidiaries to personally visit dealers. Engineers and managers from headquarters also visit Lexus dealers in the United States in order to understand their reality.

The Toyota and Lexus dealer communication network is also supported by a variety of meetings. These include National Dealer Meetings, Fireside Chat Meetings, the National Dealer Advisory Council, and the Lexus Dealer Advertising (LDA) Association. The most intensive are the Fireside Chat and National Dealer Advisory Council. The Lexus Division regards these meetings as a pair, each supplementing the other. The opinions gathered by the council reflect the majority views of dealers. Opinions and comments at Fireside Chats cover details and points that might otherwise be missed.

The objective of Fireside Chats is to discuss anything and everything regarding the company, face to face. Held in January and February, each chat involves 10 to 20 dealers. The head of the Lexus Division at TMS and operational executives meet dealer CEOs and other executives. The Lexus Division explains its policies on product pricing, marketing, and service. Using these policies as the base agenda, dealers and Lexus Division managers sit at the same table for unrestricted discussions. This is more than a simple communication of policy from the Lexus Division: the meetings are focused on listening to dealer opinions and questions. These meetings are conducted in a "we are here to listen" spirit. They began in 1995 amid the sales slump, to reduce dealer apprehension, plan solutions, and ensure future growth.

The National Dealer Advisory Council meets twice a year. Each is a three-day meeting involving nine representatives of the local dealer associations and four area office representatives. The purpose is to gather the opinions of the region and make requests to TMS. The meetings draw attention because every comment, no matter how seemingly trivial, is published in a booklet, together with TMS' response, for distribution to all dealers.

Toyota makes the annual dealer meeting a special experience for dealers by having the chair, president, and other senior executives from the headquarters in Japan present as guests, which signals that the dealers are very important for the company. Headquarters management routinely attend dealer meetings in Japan, but this is not common for the U.S. meetings of other Japanese carmakers. For U.S. car makers, the highest-ranking representative from the head office is usually the director of the division. The meetings include both Lexus and other Toyota dealers, so attendance involves 600 to 800 dealer representatives.

The Relational Dimension

Lexus dealers generally express their opinions in a very honest and constructive way. When groups have contradictory, or even just distinctive, identities, there may be barriers to information sharing, learning, and knowledge creation (Nahapiet and Ghoshal 1998).

Dealers voice opinions if they perceive system-level improvements as being in their interest. Thus, the more that dealers identify with the franchise, the more likely they are to share their knowledge (including know-how). In a survey by a national dealer association, Lexus dealers showed consistent and exceptionally high satisfaction with Toyota. This implies high identification with the car company. Although economic success has contributed to the satisfaction rating, the company's consistent acknowledgment that "there is no prosperity for a carmaker without dealers" certainly enhanced it.

Dealers need to trust in their relationship with a carmaker and with other dealers in order to share knowledge. They also need to feel they are being treated fairly. Allocation is the most significant tool for rewarding and punishing dealers, so how many high-demand vehicles a dealer can obtain makes a big difference to a dealer's business. One mechanism Toyota employs to build trust is to make the allocation process transparent. This means the formula used is objective and known to all the dealers, although they are not told each other's allocations or sales.

The Cognitive Dimension

Shared language helps participants of a network organization share thinking processes and ways of doing business. For example, area offices produce local dealer rankings and disclose the information to the dealers, without dealer names. This provides a common language to evaluate dealer performance; helps dealers share how the business should be managed; and relate to each other in terms of various performance dimensions; and encourages knowledge sharing.

Shared stories and legends help participants of the network organization share ideals, norms, and values, making it easier to create, disseminate, and maintain superior practices with less monitoring and mechanical control and fewer monetary incentives.

Lexus has been greatly helped by having a very good product. Its first offering, the LS400, became a legend for its noiseless, smooth ride and detailed craftsmanship. Other luxury carmakers are said to have disassembled it to see how it was built. The car and its legend inspired Lexus associates and dealers. This inspired pride and, as a manager in charge of Lexus service noted, "Pride in the cars leads to service quality and employee passion. I believe that the commitment to do the right thing for the customer arises from this passion and pride" (Osono 2002, pp. 13–14).

Not sharing ideals or expectations leads organizations to be less active in improvement and innovations. It leads to compromises, which is what happened at one factory that manufactures both Lexus and other Toyota cars. After introduction of the Lexus RX300, the 1999 initial quality study of new cars conducted by J. D. Power and Associates ranked the Lexus line sixth. Previously, Lexus models had been first or second. Analyzing the problem, the project leader concluded there was a lack of understanding of customer expectations among the manufacturing people, including the factory workers, and that this was a root cause.

Few of the manufacturing people in Japan had ever met a Lexus customer. They had no idea how they lived and what they required of their cars. Without a clear understanding of customer ideals and requirements, and with pressures for greater efficiency, it was easy to make compromises on quality or determine that it was impossible to achieve the required level of quality. This was reinforced by the fact that most Lexus cars were produced on the same line as cars with quality requirements lower than those of a Lexus.

To share customer expectations with the factory workers, Lexus dealers were invited to Japan. Pictures of Lexus owners and their comments were posted in the factory.

Language influences perceptions, and sharing common language helps people share perspectives, so coining a term to express Lexus quality would have been helpful. "Relentless pursuit of perfection," the tagline of the television commercial used when Lexus was introduced, could have been used, but it was not shared by the factory workers.

Group-think is a risk within a network organization that has a coherent cognitive system. For Lexus, having dealers that face different local markets helps keep the network open to new information and internally generated challenges to complacency. Meetings organized with an attentive listening attitude on the part of senior executives also helps.

Beyond Continuous Improvement

How can a network organization adapt to environmental changes that might require its participants to behave against their shared values or change their relationships? For systemic change to take place, it must be initiated by the participant central to the system. Toyota has successfully introduced other systemic changes besides creation of the Lexus Division, and some insights can be drawn from the experiences.

Introduction of the Scion in the United States was one such attempt. Toyota was trying to change its approach from "push" to "pull" by encouraging buyers to customize their cars and by changing the car-purchasing experience. ("Push" refers generally to a carmaker preferring to sell a car already built, and particularly to a dealer prefering to sell from the inventory on the lot rather than having to obtain a vehicle from another dealer or order it from the factory. The result can be to pressure a would-be buyer to choose from what is immediately available. "Pull" is letting customers choose what they like without strong pressure to select certain models.) This is systemic change. It is hard to imagine that a single dealer alone could initiate change on this scale.

In the United States, buying a car has generally been considered an unpleasant experience. Even Toyota customers had viewed it as negative. To address this, for the Scion, Toyota eliminated price negotiation and encouraged assigning a "case manager" to work with a customer through the entire process of demonstrating the vehicle, closing the sale, and arranging finance, registration, and insurance. At many competitors, these steps can involve as many as four people.

The systemic-level view must be shared with the participants. Toyota established regional headquarters in Europe and Asia, and allowed them to allocate vehicles, advertising budget, and personnel. This replaced a country-level autonomous distributor approach. Local autonomy encourages entrepreneurship in each country. However, because Toyota's way of doing business is consensus-based, it was difficult to allocate investments to specific countries, as compared to companies that use top-down decision making. Autonomy became especially problematic as Toyota faced the emerging opportunities and threats of regional free trade zones. Toyota was able to change local perspectives by sharing systemic issues among managers working in each country, and making decision making transparent.

Can This Be Transplanted?

It is not easy to develop a good network organization that continuously improves and renews itself. Examples from Toyota's operations indicate that even Toyota cannot always succeed. However, this does not mean that change is impossible.

In Thailand, dealers at one time considered Toyota an adversary, and a source of cash incentives or other promotional offers. They routinely hid retail information from Toyota Motor Thailand (TMT) in order to shift negotiations to their advantage (Osono 2003). The dealers did not contribute to the system, nor was there much mutual learning between them and TMT. Beginning in 1994, TMT undertook to change this situation. It took until 2002, but TNT was able to successfully transform the characteristics of its network organization with local Toyota dealers.

First, TMT had to change the norm from making profits out of cash incentives and promotional funds to making profits by satisfying customers. To satisfy customers and minimize opportunity loss, better logistics management had to be introduced, and, for this, retail sales information had to be shared between dealers and TMT. TMT increased face-to-face communication. TMT also shared a new business model with the dealers. This was the "customer first, dealer second, and factory [including TMT] last" approach used elsewhere. Then, TMT established clear rules, especially regarding allocation. By establishing stable policies and firm rules regarding order and delivery, the allocation system was made more transparent and less political, enabling the dealers to see its integrity.

TMT also provided advice and process management tools. It adopted a listening attitude, and changed the network from sparse to dense, making mutual learning easier. Overall, TMT established camaraderie. Operations became one of continuous improvement and mutual learning. The vision for Thailand has become the strategic core of Toyota's strategy for developing countries.

Conclusion

The Lexus network organization, which consists of Toyota Motor Corporation, TMS Lexus Division, and Lexus dealers, has the following characteristics.

In terms of performance, continuous improvement occurs in various places within the network organization. Improvements are shared and stay within the organization. As a result, the organization consistently has outperformed competitors in a very competitive environment.

In terms of social assets, the network organization provides incentives and motivation for each participant to improve by allowing participants to enjoy autonomy and to take initiative. Participants are motivated to share knowledge because of mutual trust and a reciprocal relationship. They perceive that they benefit from shared information, including helping other dealers improve.

The structural dimension contributes to this. A stable membership, a small number of participants, and multiple layers of communication provide participants with opportunities to exchange tacit knowledge and learning. It is a dense, intensive communication network through which tacit knowledge such as norms, values, and visions is shared. As a result, participants identify with the organization. This discourages opportunistic behavior. Having Toyota positioned at the center of the network enables it to proactively search for the innovations taking place in the peripheral areas of the community.

These characteristics were developed by Toyota's consistent and continuous investment in social capital in order to strengthen the network. Developing a system that self-improves and self-renews requires time and consistent effort and investment in social assets. Without a long-term commitment and consistency, it is not possible to create a continuously improving group of organizations.

Successful application of the network organization structure means continuous learning and an innovation process shared among group members. The benefit is an upgrading of organizational capabilities at each participating company and for the group as a whole.

References

Allen, Thomas J. 1977. *Managing The Flow of Technology.* MIT Press, Cambridge, Mass.

Dyer, Jeffrey H., and Nile W. Hatch. 2004. "Using Supplier Networks to Learn Faster." *MIT Sloan Management Review* (Spring): 57–63.

Garvin, David A. 1993. "Building A Learning Organization." *Harvard Business Review* (July–August): 78–91.

Ghoshal, Sumantra, Christopher A. Bartlett and Peter Moran. 1999. "A New Manifesto for Management." *Sloan Management Review* 40–3: 9–20.

Liker, Jeffrey K., and Tohmas Y. Choi. 2004. "Building Deep Supplier Relationships." *Harvard Business Review* (December): 104–113.

Nahapiet, Janine, and Sumantra Ghoshal. 1998. "Social Capital, Intellectual Capital, and The Organizational Advantage." *Academy of Management Review* 23: 242–266.

Nonaka, Ikujiro, and Hirotaka Takeuchi. 1995. *The Knowledge Creating Company.* New York: Oxford University Press.

Nonaka, Ikujiro and Ryoko Toyama. 2005. "The Theory of The Knowledge-Creating Firm: Subjectivity, Objectivity and Synthesis." *Industrial and Corporate Change* 14: 419–436.

Osono, Emi. 2002. *Lexus: Toyota's Challenge of The U.S. Luxury Car Market.* ICS case series, Hitotsubashi University.

Osono, Emi. 2003. *Toyota Motor Corporation Asia: A Historical Challenge.* ICS case series, Hitotsubashi University.

Osono, Emi. 2004a. *Can Toyota Attract Young Customers? (B): Birth of Scion.* ICS case series, Hitotsubashi University.

Osono, Emi. 2004b. "The Strategy Making Process as Dialogue," in Hirotaka Takeuchi and Ikujiro Nonaka. *Hitotsubashi on Knowledge Management.* Singapore: John Wiley & Sons.

Prusak, Laurence, and Don Cohen. 2001. "How to Invest in Social Capital." *Harvard Business Review* (June): 108–118.

Rogers, Everett M. 1995. *Diffusion of Innovations.* New York: Free Press.

Tsai, Wenpin, and Smantra Ghoshal. 1998. "Social Capital and Value Creation: The Role of Intrafirm Networks." *Academy of Management Review* 41: 464–476.

4

Strategic Management of Knowledge-Based Competence: Sharp Corporation

Kazuo Ichijo

In the knowledge-based economy, individual and organizational knowledge, as well as brainpower, have replaced physical assets as critical resources in the corporate world (Drucker 1993). Therefore, the success of a company in the 21st century is determined by the extent to which its leaders can develop intellectual capabilities through knowledge creation and sharing. Knowledge constitutes a competitive advantage (Eisenhardt and Santos 2001). Companies should hire, develop, and retain excellent managers who accumulate precious knowledge assets. Attracting smart, talented people and raising their level of intellectual capabilities is a core competency.

At the same time, companies should encourage proficient managers to share the knowledge they develop across geographical and functional boundaries in an effective, efficient, and fast manner. In other words, to win in the competitive environment, companies need to be able to manage knowledge strategically. That means management of knowledge should also constitute a core competency. This is especially the case for companies doing business outside their domestic market. However, despite various efforts, few firms succeeded in increasing their knowledge assets.

Since the early 1990s, "knowledge management" has been a hot issue. Business researchers, consultants, and journalists from all over the world suggest that companies focus on developing knowledge workers (engineers, software designers, scientists, doctors, writers, and creative thinkers) to build a learning environment that will meet the demands of the postindustrial information economy and win in the competitive global setting.

Globalization means firms are affected by what happens beyond their national borders. This is an opportunity as well as a challenge. Companies globalize their operations for several compelling reasons.

- By locating manufacturing operations where factor costs are low, firms can gain a cost advantage.
- By working closely with advanced and demanding customers in some markets, firms can acquire valuable information, experience, and knowledge for product development.
- By having operations abroad, companies can gain better access to growing foreign markets. Sometimes this is done with a local partner. Sometimes it is driven by the necessity of attracting good local managers.
- By locating R&D facilities in countries with well-developed educational and scientific traditions, firms gain access to expertise, technologies, and product concepts.

Given stiff global competition and rapid technological change, the way firms manage their knowledge assets drives key competitive factors. In fields with constant technological changes, manufacturers need to both develop new technologies and focus on protecting their expertise from competitors (Doz et al. 2001). Furthermore, managers have to relentlessly pursue activities to keep from having obsolete technologies. For these reasons, decision-making issues concerning knowledge-based competence of a corporation are becoming broader and more diverse.

In much of the literature, the discussion of executing knowledge management within corporations has overemphasized creative and sharing activities. These activities occur consistently only if there is a sufficient infrastructure within the organization to consistently enable them (Von Krogh et al. 2000). Knowledge management should be understood more holistically. To that end, this chapter presents a case study of the Sharp Corporation.

The chapter is organized as follows. The next section introduces Sharp and provides background on the liquid crystal display (LCD) market in which it competes. The company's strategy is then taken up. In particular, the case of LCD televisions is looked at in detail. From this practical application of the holistic knowledge vision concept, some general theoretical and management implications are drawn.

Gaining and Sustaining Competitive Advantage

Companies facing stiff competition should develop holistic views of knowledge management. A case in point is Sharp and its "black box" knowledge asset. That means making a company's unique knowledge difficult to imitate. This is done using a combination of factors such as product customization, complexity, and intellectual property protection. Sharp has endorsed this as the keystone of its corporate strategy.

Sharp is one of the best-performing electronics manufacturers in Japan. In fiscal year 2004 (ended March 2005), consolidated sales reached ¥2.53 trillion (12% greater than in fiscal 2003), operating profit was ¥150 billion (up 23%) and net income was ¥75 billion (up 24%). While other Japanese electronics firms have been struggling with falling sales, Sharp's performance has been outstanding.

This success was mainly brought about by LCD devices and related products. For example, in 2002 Sharp was the first to introduce mobile phones with cameras. Creation of this market was possible because of Sharp's development of the necessary components.

Head-to-Head Competition in Asia

Sharp has become a leading global electronics manufacturer by cultivating new frontiers using its LCD technologies. LCDs were developed by Radio Corporation of America (RCA) in 1963, and in 1968 RCA made the first LCD panel. However, due to manufacturing difficulties, RCA and other U.S. companies gave up commercialization.

Sharp, on the other hand, identified growth opportunities in the business and took the lead in exploiting LCD technologies for innovative products. The first was a small calculator with a black and white LCD, introduced in 1973. PDAs (personal digital assistants) and camcorders followed. Sharp's strategy was to continuously and relentlessly improve LCD technology in order to cultivate new LCD product markets. As a result, Sharp has become the industrial leader.

Developing ever-larger LCD panels posed a technological challenge. In 1988, Sharp succeeded in building a 14.4-inch LCD panel for PCs.

In the 1990s, LCDs gradually began to replace CRT (cathode ray tube) monitors as PC monitors. As a result, Taiwanese LCD manufacturers emerged as strong competitors. Many U.S. PC makers outsource manufacturing to companies in Taiwan, China, so firms such as Unipac Optoelectronics Corp. were established to produce LCDs. One of their competitive advantages was being able to collaborate with leading PC makers such as International Business Machines Corp. (IBM). This meant they could produce appropriate monitors with shorter delays at a much cheaper cost.

Taiwanese firms simply purchased the same production equipment being sold to Sharp and other Japanese LCD manufacturers. They were especially competitive in producing smaller panels for PC displays. In contrast, Japanese firms were more interested in bigger panels so that they could produce monitors much more efficiently. The leading Taiwanese LCD manufacturers, Unipac and ADT (Acer Display Technology), merged in 2001 and became AU Optronics (AUO).

Korean competitors include Samsung Electronics and LG Electronics. Samsung is a particularly challenging competitor. The company was left with a huge debt burden following the 1997 Korean financial crisis, a crash in memory-chip prices, and a $700 million write-off related to the takeover AST Technologies, a U.S. maker of PCs. Samsung Group Chair Lee Kun-Hee, the son of the group's founder and its head since 1987, brought in a new CEO Yun Jong in 1996. They saw a turnaround opportunity in the shift from analog to digital, and undertook a radical transformation of Samsung. Speed and intelligence would be key success factors in the new digitized electronics industry. Samsung rationalized its operations, selling businesses considered noncore for $2 billion. This, together with other job cuts, reduced employment by 24,000.

To gain profitability, Samsung focused exclusively on fast-growing digital products and devices such as LCDs, plasma displays, cell phones, digital cameras, and flash memories. Competing through speed in new product development, manufacturing launches, and economies of scale was to be its winning strategy. (For more on the company's remake, see *Business Week* 2003.)

Samsung has become a fast mover in the LCD business. It had always lagged Sharp in LCD panel launches. However, it surprised the public by bringing the fifth generation of LCD panels to market in mid-2003, well ahead of Sharp. (LCD panel generations relate to their size; the fifth was 1,100 × 1,250 mm.)

Sharp's Strategy for the LCD Business

Although it faced tougher competition from companies such as AUO, Samsung, and LG electronics, Sharp has not changed its strategy: always be a technological leader.

In 2002, Sharp succeeded in developing continuous grain (CG) silicon liquid crystals. It was the first technology to create and control crystal particles that could be made into thin layers and attached to glass. This meant a simple glass board could be transformed into an LCD panel or television screen. Moreover, it had the capability of storing TV programs by operating semiconductor memories inside. CG silicon has the advantage of providing a clearer display compared to other LCDs. Moreover, it is possible to arrange the display and related devices on the same glass board. Each product can be conveniently customized according to its needs. The technology is being used in a number of Sharp products, and panels are sold to others, including competitors producing camera cell phones.

The development was not shared even within Sharp before its release to the market. Sharp has filed for only a few patents related to CG silicon. This is very different from the usual way in the industry. For a long time, Sharp was famous for filing the largest number of LCD-related patents. Now, it emphasizes "black boxed know-how and technologies" to maintain competitiveness. The shift reflects realization that filing patents means revealing the essence of the technology to competitors.

One consequence of the shift was having to create equipment for manufacturing CG silicones inside the company. With this move, the stickiness of knowledge concerning the technology was expected to improve (von Hippel 1998). Where equipment was purchased from outside, Sharp customized it beyond recognition.

Black box knowledge requires continuous management attention to dissemination of knowledge within the company. Sharp faced a complicated chain of decisions.

1. Development of CG silicon as a result of knowledge creation;
2. Customizability of final product issues (such as avoiding the imitation of a product by potential competitors);
3. Accelerated structuring of the production process;
4. Shaping the skills of mass production and managerial techniques.

The third and fourth aimed at delaying competitor catch-up. The steps taken were strategically very effective. Only with the implementation and continuation of tightly related strategic plans could Sharp expect to remain the leader in the LCD market for mobile-sized devices—that is screens used on mobile phones and PDAs such as its own Zaurus (called Wizard in the United States).

In the 1990s Sharp saw the importance of the niche market—mobile-sized LCDs—when all the other manufacturers were focused on larger sizes. Sharp's choice may have been a result of a unique corporate policy of "achieving the top in one-of-a-kind industry." Adding to such niche positioning, the fact that mobile LCDs were often customized helped prevent products from being commoditized.

Uniqueness of knowledge is one of the effective factors that prevent technology imitations (Chakravarthy et al. 2003). This extra layer of competitive shield, brought by niche positioning and customizability, completely eliminated followers. However, in order to sustain advantage, Sharp must first utilize the knowledge created to develop innovative products and protect them effectively. The combination of strategic positioning and strategic management of knowledge-based competence of a firm is crucially important for Sharp in gaining and sustaining its competitive advantage.

CG silicon shows that layers of interrelated knowledge-based activities protect corporate knowledge assets. Sharp is now trying to change the rules of competition in the large-LCD market by applying the same line of attack. The next section looks at the case of LCD televisions in more detail in order to formulate a valid hypothesis concerning knowledge-based management.

Knowledge Vision and Innovation in the Television Market

Sharp is known for pioneering revolutionary LCD televisions, and is one of the leading players in this market. In 2004 it had a 34% global share, selling nearly 1.5 million sets. Share in Japan was almost 50% (755,000 sets), and outside Japan was almost 27% (726,000 sets). In the four years beginning in January 2001 when it introduced the Aquos series, Sharp accounted for 36% (5 million) of the 14 million LCD sets sold.

In 1998 Katsuhiko Machida, Sharp's president, announced his vision of selling only LCD sets in the Japanese market by 2005. This was only two months after he assumed the helm. Machida had long been concerned about the future of Sharp's televisions. At the time, aggressive Korean competitors were affecting the market. Although Sharp started production of 14-inch CRT sets in 1953, OEMs (original equipment manufacturers) had supplied the CRTs, and the company had continued to rely on outside sources, many of them competitors in the finished-set market.

Machida, having served as general manager of television products, foresaw the approaching loss of corporate negotiation power if TVs, the most prestigious electronics product line at the time, started to plunge. Thus, the new vision was aimed at gaining and sustaining competitive advantage in the global electronics industry. To that end, Machida was willing to discard its knowledge of how to produce CRT TV sets. This was a bold decision. Although Sharp did not produce the CRTs, it had developed considerable knowledge regarding CRT TV sets, including manufacturing processes and color coordination technologies.

At the time, Sharp had been active in development of LCDs for nearly 30 years, and had introduced the first calculator with an LCD in 1973. Still, including television in its long-term commitment to developing LCD technologies was significant. It was an aspect of Sharp's knowledge vision, because the company has always pursued innovation as an electronics company.

The vision statement was a surprise. At that time, the general belief was that tube TV sets would be the mainstream for quite a while longer. Technically, it was not easy to expand the size of an LCD panel, which made the vision a risky bet. Sony, Sharp's strongest competitor in TVs, was not willing to discard its knowledge of producing traditional CRTs, given its success with its Trinitron monitors.

Machida's knowledge-based vision statement was neither a forecast nor an outlook. It came out of definite originality. Shigemitsu Mizushima, then development manager of the LCD television project, was among those astounded by the announcement. Now general manager of the display technology development group, Mizushima did not know of the new vision until it was publicly announced. At the time, he did not have enough confidence in making LCD panels through 100% internal production. Yet, he was assigned to lead the product development team.

Previous products with LCDs, such as PC monitors, were designed for viewing from the front. Televisions required a broader viewing angle. This led the team develop a customized LCD, the Advanced Super View (ASV). Color display was another major issue. A joint project team from the LCD group, which had knowledge of high-resolution color display, and the television group, with expertise in television screen color control, was formed. Engineers from the television group in Tochigi, north of Tokyo, spontaneously joined the LCD group based in Tenri, near Osaka.

Japanese companies generally have strong functional and divisional boundaries that make cross-functional and cross-divisional activities difficult. In contrast, for Sharp, such coordination was neither new nor difficult: it had been using "Urgent Project Teams"—cross-functional task forces—since 1977. The teams had developed a number of hit products. Thus, the organization believed it was natural to work beyond one's own division. Such a culture was deeply rooted and was not easy for competitors to duplicate (Reber 1993). Machida has always praised the advantage of this tacit culture. He believed the rapid process of development and production was due to this "Urgent Project Team" tradition. The strength of the organization was built on the tacit knowledge brought about by historical organizational activities (Winter 1987).

In 2005 Sharp purchased Fujitsu Ltd.'s LCD panel operations. These had been unprofitable, and Fujitsu was looking to exit the business. Sharp also acquired ownership of some technology it previously had paid to license.

Spiral Process and "Black Box" Knowledge

Working toward the knowledge vision led the organization to further success. Sharp's market share in televisions improved from 11.5% in 1998 to 20.0% in 2003. In 2002, Sharp's LCD television revenue surpassed that of tube televisions.

The company invested ¥100 billion in a new plant with the then-latest equipment in Kameyama, in Mie prefecture between Osaka and Nagoya. All processes, from production of LCD panels to assembly of LCD TVs, are in the plant, which started operations in January 2004. The plant produces sixth-generation panels, which are 1,500 × 1,800 mm. That is large enough to make eight 30-inch LCD TVs. The plant can produce some 100,000 each month. The machine used in panel production is so large that, at first, it seemed impossible to find a road to transport it to the plant.

The Kameyama plant was a strategic initiative for Sharp, and was intended to change the rules of the LCD business. Panel size had been the key factor, with companies focusing on enlarging them. By aiming at optimization of devices and products, with the Kameyama plant project Sharp took the lead in terms of efficiency. Thus, Sharp leaped directly from fourth- to sixth-generation panels. To do this, project members reviewed technologies and processes and changed them radically. By combining the production of mother glass and the assembly of TVs in one place, Sharp was able to achieve both high speed and cost effectiveness. This exemplifies what is called the "spiral effect." Although the circuits in LCD panels and TVs differ from each other, concentrating the production site enhanced integration.

The Kameyama plant physically created the context (*ba* in Japanese) of innovation (knowledge creation), where organization members share tacit and explicit knowledge with each other through dialogue, thus facilitating cross-divisional and cross-functional coordination. The LCD technology and TV development departments had been located far apart. However, top management thought collaboration between the two was crucial in developing new LCD TVs faster, more effectively, and efficiently. Experience with ad hoc "Urgent Project Teams" allowed cross-divisional and cross-functional coordination on a permanently institutionalized level in Kameyama.

One Kameyama-based engineer in LCD technology development commented, "It is so exciting to see the process of LCD TV development just on the spot. I am so happy to see new LCDs I had developed are assembled into TV sets just in front of me" (interview by author, January 15, 2004). As this shows, the social relationship among engineers in the two departments has improved. This is an important part of *ba*, and a key enabler for knowledge creation.

An innovative mix of novel LCD development and manufacturing technology with TV production technology also created an important barrier of complexity. This protects Sharp from being imitated. As the value chain premise indicates, the more different activities are linked, the higher the value that can be created. Increased complexity makes technology difficult to copy (Simon 1962).

When plans for Kameyama were announced in 2002, production was expected to start in May 2004. However, rapid growth of the LCD television market led to accelerated actions: production began in January 2004. Sharp had launched another plant in Mie in June 2003. There it tested various activities. These experiences were used in building in Kameyama, and the plant is called the "knowledge integrated building."

In January 2005 Sharp announced plans to build a ¥150 billion plant adjacent to the existing one in Kameyama to build eighth-generation panels (2,160 × 2,400 mm) usable in 40- and 50-inch TV sets. It is expected to open in October 2006.

Theoretical and Management Implications

This section uses Sharp's example to summarize the activities that enhanced making use of knowledge assets in an organization in order to gain and sustain a competitive advantage. Discussions of strategic management of knowledge assets tend to focus on creation of and sharing the knowledge assets. However, the Sharp case suggests the necessity for a more holistic view.

Holistic Knowledge Management

Holistic knowledge management consists of four main activities: creating, sharing, protecting, and discarding.

Creating. Companies should be knowledge-creating companies, trying to generate new knowledge well ahead of competitors (Nonaka and Takeuchi 1995). Sharp is a knowledge-creating company, and it has always taken the lead in innovation in the global LCD business.

Sharing. After successfully creating new knowledge within a company, it has to be shared among organizational members across regions, businesses, and functions. Sharp shows excellence at cross-functional and cross-divisional knowledge sharing. Without active knowledge sharing, Sharp would not have become the number-one player in the LCD television business.

Protecting. This means keeping the firm's knowledge assets out of the hands of competitors. Sharp has put tremendous effort into making imitation of its LCD TV sets time-consuming and difficult. Various initiatives at Kameyama are aimed at increasing complexities and tacitness of knowledge in order to make imitation extremely difficult.

Discarding. Companies need to reflect on whether their knowledge is outdated. In some cases, it may be necessary to discard existing knowledge and promote new knowledge creation. Indeed, without discarding old knowledge, the creation of new knowledge is difficult to initiate. Sharp discarded various kinds of knowledge about producing CRT TV sets in shifting to LCD TVs. In contrast, Sony stuck with Trinitron tubes and lost competitive advantage. Note that Sony was an industrial leader in CRT TVs, Sharp was not. As the leader in LCD technology, it might be harder for Sharp to discard its knowledge than when it was not the technology leader. However, being ready to discard technology is how to avoid the "innovator's dilemma" (Christensen 1997). When the time comes that LCD technologies are obsolete, Sharp should not be afraid to discard its outdated knowledge.

So as not to be stuck with obsolete knowledge, Sharp is pursuing research on technologies that could replace LCDs in certain products. These include electro-

Figure 4.1.   *Strategic Management of Knowledge-Based Competence of a Firm*

Strategic Management of Knowledge

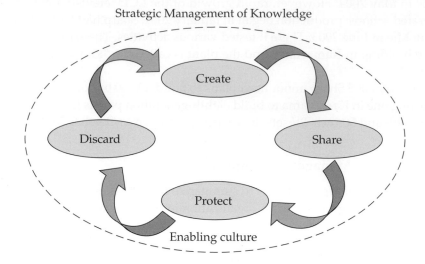

luminescence. By developing alternatives itself, Sharp can prevent being leap-frogged by competitors.

Solar cells were made a second core business in January 2005. Sharp began solar energy research in 1959, and has been among the leaders in the industry. It started mass-producing panels in 1963 and in 1980 introduced a a solar-powered calculator. This is part of a broader strategy to be among the most environmentally friendly companies in the world. Thus, LCDs use less energy than plasma displays, while the solar panels generate energy.

Making Imitation Difficult

Preventing knowledge from being imitated is about activities that increase "complexity," "tacitness," and "specialty." The maintenance of enabling conditions is indispensable for facilitating these activities. Sharing a mission and vision throughout an organization, a unique strategy to attain them, an organizational culture that promotes knowledge creation and sharing, and leadership to initiate building strong competitiveness are all necessary enabling conditions. Such building blocks of knowledge management are linked. In short, it is very important to make them influence one another to allow knowledge assets to reach full potential.

Although the boundaries between knowledge creation and organizational learning are sometimes vague, they are usually considered separate activities. The holistic view of knowledge-based competence of a corporation is free from this dichotomy. Organizations store knowledge both by knowledge-creating activities stimulated by new personal experiences and by organizational learning activities, produced by others' experiences (Chakravarthy et al. 2003).

Organizational learning plays an essential role in the storing process of knowledge (Argyris 1992). In an age of rapid technological change, it is important for organizations to learn from competitors. This may seem a contradiction given the earlier discussion of the risks of technological imitation. However, organizations can easily fall into the "not invented here" syndrome, where they end up believing exclusively in their own technologies and products, and often reject or ignore those of competitors.

Failures can provide as many useful lessons as successes. For example, if quality problems cause dissolution of a competing enterprise, one can grasp the importance of quality control activities in the market. Without a doubt, analysis must be both outside and inside the organization. This is because a company can learn from the mistakes of other companies.

Conclusion

To cultivate a new business frontier, companies need to gain and maintain competitive advantage. This requires taking the lead in developing new technologies and producing innovative products and services using these technologies. Simply, knowledge creation matters. To avoid catch-up by competitors, companies must be good at utilizing new technologies for various business opportunities, as well as protecting their technologies from imitation. Therefore, knowledge sharing and protection are of importance in sustaining competitive advantage. Yet, any technology ultimately becomes obsolete. Companies that have led by developing core technologies tend to be especially late in developing and using new technologies that may supersede their incumbent technologies. To accomplish sustained growth, firms must avoid the innovator's dilemma. This means being willing to discard the knowledge of previous core technologies.

To catch new business opportunities before competitors, and to keep that advantage as long as possible, it is indispensable to protect and defend knowledge that leads to innovation. Management of knowledge assets has to go further than simple technology management. Asserting knowledge ownership by acquiring patents is not enough. The time has come to move toward holistic knowledge-based management.

That means those who intend to gain and sustain advantage in a rapidly moving environment must pay more attention to the importance of creating, sharing, protecting, and discarding knowledge. These activities must be executed consistently. All four are important in consistently improving a firm's intellectual assets.

For companies in advanced countries, discarding knowledge can be difficult because of the long history of knowledge creation. Old knowledge dies hard. The more success a company has had, the more difficult it is to discard knowledge it has created. In contrast, for companies in developing countries, the absence of legacy knowledge is a potential source of competitive advantage. Such firms might be able to create or exploit new knowledge well ahead of established competitors.

As the shift from analog to digital technologies has shown, there are many opportunities for companies in developing countries. They should not think small. Be a knowledge-creating company. This is a strong message to companies in developing countries.

References

Argyris, Chris. 1992. *On Organizational Learning.* Oxford: Blackwell.

Business Week. 2003, June 16. "The Samsung Way." p. 46–53.

Chakravarthy, Bala, Sue McEvily, Yves Doz, and Devaki Rau. 2003. "Knowledge Management and Competitive Advantage." In M. Easterby-Smith and M. A. Lyles, editors, *The Blackwell Handbook of Organizational Learning and Knowledge Management,* 205-323. Oxford: Blackwell Publishing.

Christensen, Clayton. 1997. *Innovator's Dilemma: When New technologies Cause Great Firms to Fail.* Boston, MA: Harvard Business School Press.

Doz, Yves L., José F. P. Santos, and Peter J. Williamson. 2001. *From Global to Metanational: How Companies Win in the Knowledge Economy.* Boston, MA: Harvard Business School Press.

Drucker, Peter F. 1993. *Post-Capitalist Society.* New York: HarperCollins.

Eisenhardt, Kathleen M., and José F. P. Santos. 2001. "Knowledge-Based View: A New Theory of Strategy." In Andrew M. Pettigrew, Thomas Howard, and Richard Whitington, editors, *Handbook of Strategy and Management.* London: Sage Publications.

Garvin, David A. 1993. Building a Learning Organization. In *Harvard Business Review on Knowledge Management.* Boston, MA: Harvard Business School Press.

Nonaka, Ikujiro, and Hirotaka Takeuchi. 1995. *The Knowledge-Creating Company: How Japanese Companies Create the Dynamics of Innovation.* New York: Oxford University Press.

Reber, Arthur S. 1993. *Implicit Learning and Tacit Knowledge: An Essay on the Cognitive Unconscious.* New York: Oxford University Press.

Simon, Herbert A. 1962. "The Architecture of Complexity." *Proceedings of the American Philosophical Society* 106: 467–82.

Von Hippel, Edgar. 1998. *Sources of Innovation.* New York: Oxford University Press.

Von Krogh, Georg, Kazuo Ichijo, and Ikujiro Nonaka. 2000. *Enabling Knowledge Creation: How to Unlock the Mystery of Tacit Knowledge and Release the Power of Innovation.* New York: Oxford University Press.

Winter, Sidney G. 1987. "Knowledge and Competence as Strategic Assets." In David Teece, editor, *The Competitive Challenge: Strategies for Industrial Innovation and Renewal.* New York: Harper and Row.

5

Invisible Dimensions of Differentiation: Japanese Electronics Companies

Ken Kusunoki

There are only two ways to increase profits: reduce costs or boost customer willingness to pay (WTP). In the face of the intense competition that has been squeezing profit margins, companies have tried various best practices to maintain profitability. These include restructuring with a focus on core businesses, business process re-engineering, outsourcing, information technology (IT)–driven supply chain management (SCM) initiatives, and globalization.

These efforts are fundamentally focused on reducing cost. Although cost reduction is important, it is insufficient to maintain continuous profitability increases. By its very definition, cost-based competition converges on the physical limits of cost and price, and ultimately is a dead end. Companies focused exclusively on reducing costs ultimately hang themselves with their own rope. Firms must increase customer WTP in order to gain profitability.

While many firms strive to reduce costs, only a few succeed in increasing WTP. This is because, in general, reducing costs is "simpler" than raising WTP—not that it is an easy task to undercut rivals in terms of cost. But, it is certainly easier to undertake cost reductions than to increase WTP.

One key underlying factor is commoditization. The essence of competition is doing things differently from competitors, and it is difficult to create differences once a product or service becomes a commodity. Price becomes the only differentiator a firm can show customers. Commoditization, therefore, means competition converges on cost.

This chapter focuses on Japan's electronics industry and suggests strategies for overcoming commoditization and creating customer WTP. The conclusions are summarized in three points.

- Value-dimension visibility is the key concept for understanding commoditization. Commoditization can be understood as the process by which the value dimensions of a product or service become increasingly visible to consumers as technology and markets mature.
- Creating differentiation along invisible value dimensions is a possible strategy for escaping commoditization. This nondimensional differentiation seeks to drive WTP in the external context of the customer interface by disrupting the very rules of dimensional competition and transforming competition into something nondimensional.
- Achieving nondimensional differentiation requires new types of knowledge and the management to create that knowledge.

Digitization, Modularization, and Commoditization

The speed at which products and services can become commodities has dramatically increased since the late 1980s. The trend is particularly remarkable in the electronics industry, which includes data communications as well as electronic equipment and devices.

Why? Because the industry has been subject to modularization, globalization, and conversion to open systems. All of these reflect rapid digitization. Digitization means encoding analog data (by definition, continuous) into discrete (discontinuous) values—specifically, the binary code used by computers. The essence of IT progress lies in the dramatically lower cost of handling highly flexible digitized information.

Digitization affects products and services as systems. That is, it affects their architectures, and does so in a number of ways. Modularization of architectures is the most fundamental of these changes.

Architecture defines how to break a system down into components, and how those components are linked in subsystem interdependencies. It is a concept for understanding system states. Modularization means breaking down an entire system into multiple groups (modules), each of which consists of a number of highly interdependent subsystems, with predefined rules regarding the interface between modules. It can also be defined as a strategy for minimizing system complexity and relational interdependence between structural components by anticipating and solving beforehand the problems that arise when modules interact.

The personal computer (PC) is the world's most modularized product system. The functions a PC must perform—calculation, short-term memory, long-term memory, input, display, and so forth—are allocated to the central processing unit (CPU), random access memory (RAM), hard drive, keyboard, monitor, and other physical components. A standardized interface intermediates component interaction.

Modularization drives the trend toward open system architectures. Open architecture refers to systems for which subsystem interface rules are publicly disclosed and widely accepted. Modularized systems are easier to convert to open systems because their interface rules tend to be simpler. And when architecture becomes open, the number of people who can be involved immediately expands, making it easier for the company to enjoy outsourcing, network externality, and economy of scale benefits. Thanks to modularization, companies are able to lower costs in ways never before possible.

Ironically, these trends also work to accelerate commoditization. A completely open, modularized architecture promotes efficiency at the macroeconomic level. But at the individual corporate level, sharing standardized rules enables competitors to enter the market. Inevitably, when products and services cannot be differentiated, the result is price competition.

This describes today's PC industry. Firms pursuing modularization have specialized, either focusing on individual software or hardware modules or becoming final assemblers of components. When the industry was immature, the benefits of modularization drove product development, enhanced efficiency, and expanded the market. But as PC technology matured, most companies specialized in individual modules became unable to differentiate on any dimension other than price.

When modularization is complete, it even becomes impossible to add value based on effectively combining components at the design and assembly phases, a process

Figure 5.1. *Profitability of Major Japanese Electronics Companies, 1994–2003*

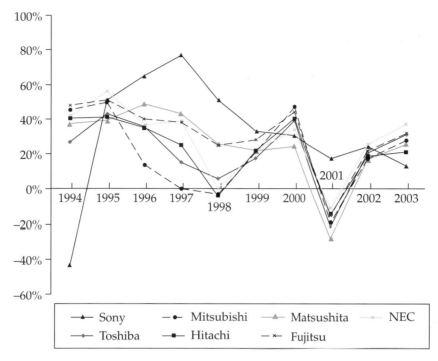

Data are for fiscal years ending in March of the following calendar year.
Profitability is measured as parent-company operating profits as a percent of sales.
Source: Annual reports.

called optimization through mutual adjustment. That's because interface rules have
already solved the problems of coordinating the assembly of different components.

Thus, modularization drives commoditization. And, to the extent a product or
service is a commodity, buyers focus solely on price. Thus, modularization has had
negative consequences, especially for the Japanese electronics giants, because they
have been more vertically and horizontally integrated companies. In the analog era,
these companies could derive economies of scope and scale out of their integral
business architectures. Digitization and modularization eventually made such integral advantages insignificant. As further discussed in volume 1, chapter 5, these
large firms lost ground to companies focused on specific modules.

Figure 5.1 shows how leading diversified Japanese electronics manufacturers'
operating incomes have changed since the mid-1990s. Several trends are apparent. First, most firms had operating income of less than 4% of sales. Second, while
fluctuating, the level has been trending downward. Third, with the exception of
Sony, the levels are extremely uniform, particularly since 1999. These facts suggest that the leading firms in Japan's electronics sector have lapsed into competitive convergence. They suffer from low profitability and are unable to establish
clearly differentiated positions that set them apart from rivals.

Value-Dimension Visibility and its Dynamics

To devise decommoditization strategies, one must understand the logic of commoditization. The key is value-dimension visibility. Both customers and companies

understand product and service value in terms of a few specific dimensions. Competition and differentiation can be broadly divided into dimensional and nondimensional. This can also be called "competition and differentiation along visible dimensions" and "competition and differentiation along invisible dimensions."

Conventional thinking about competitive strategy assumes competition and differentiation are dimensional phenomena. In other words, they progress along clearly defined measures of value. PC industry competition in the 1990s is a typical case. Companies and their customers widely shared specific, easily comprehensible, and objective measures of functionality: processing speed, memory size, monitor resolution, and the like. In that environment, differentiation meant outdistancing rivals along one of these measures. Competition centered on the relative advantages each firm enjoyed along readily comparable dimensions.

In contrast, the music, game software, and fashion industries provide classic examples of competition along invisible dimensions. Industries like these have experienced many innovations. Sun Records' release of Elvis Presley's rock-and-roll music, Enix's Dragon Quest role-playing game, and Swatch's fashion watches are all innovations that created high WTP.

With innovations like these, it is difficult to specify precise dimensions along which the product or service improved on predecessors. The music Elvis Presley created had a faster tempo compared to pop music of the time. But the essence of Elvis's "difference" was not that he exceeded Frank Sinatra in terms of number of beats per measure. Swatch watches were not more accurate or durable compared to rival products. They were available in greater variety, but even variety was not the dimension along which Swatch created new value. These products definitely were different compared to conventional music and watches, but it is difficult to grasp by what measure they were different.

Value-dimension visibility varies depending on the product or service. A more critical point is that it is not constant, even for a single industry or product. Value-dimension visibility rises and falls as industries and products evolve. Although the dynamics vary, in most industries it is possible to observe common patterns (Figure 5.2).

Figure 5.2.   *Dynamics of Visibility of Value Dimensions*

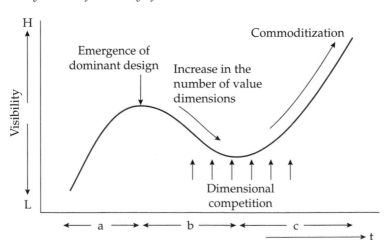

PCs as an Example

The dynamics of value-dimension visibility can be illustrated by the PC industry. At the initial stage of an industry's development, before a dominant design has been established, value visibility is normally low. When the PC industry was in its infancy, nonbusiness users were largely "techies" and "geeks." At that stage, both manufacturers and users lacked a common understanding of exactly what the PC's basic value was, and what functions were critical to defining that value. In other words, the personal computer's value dimensions were not very visible.

Dominant design establishment means a consensus formed concerning a PC's value. Once IBM and Apple had established dominant designs, PC values could be understood along a limited number of specific dimensions. In other words, the process of establishing a dominant design is the same as the process of raising value visibility. This is stage "a" in Figure 5.2. PC hardware innovations were quite dimensional, and companies plunged into an era of competition along specific dimensions.

Users gradually deepened their product understanding and expanded uses in the workplace and home. New buyers using PCs for a wider variety of applications entered the market. As the industry moved into the 1990s, PC makers sought to differentiate not merely by price and speed, but along a wide range of value dimensions: body and monitor size, RAM and hard drive capacity, durability, varied functionality, user support, and postsale services.

This can be described as the trend toward a multiplicity of value dimensions. At this stage, the number of value dimensions had broadened considerably compared to the early days. This served to lower value specifiability and universality for both users and manufacturers, which consequently lowered value visibility ("b" in Figure 5.2).

However value-dimension visibility starts to rise again if competition continues along the various dimensions ("c" in Figure 5.2). This is because, under dimensional competition, the respective value dimensions ultimately achieve levels deemed satisfactory by customers. Makers emulate each other's innovations and, one by one, the dimensions along which competitors can differentiate disappear. Once specifications along each dimension reach levels satisfactory to nearly every customer, further innovation, even if technologically possible, fails to produce new value.

Growth in the PC sector, which averaged 15% annually through the 1990s, slowed starting in 2000, then suddenly dropped. In 2001, only 11% of users considered buying a new PC, the lowest level since 1995. This was not because the need for PCs had fallen. Rather, the PC's various functions had reached levels sufficient to satisfy nearly every user. Indeed, PCs are loaded to the brim with unused functions. Thus, customers no longer see any added value in new products, with the result that there is little reason to replace machines. Quite simply, current PCs are "good enough": Further dimensional differentiation does nothing but invoke price wars.

Under these conditions, price is the only remaining visible dimension along which companies can attempt to differentiate. This is commoditization, where value visibility is highest. It is, in short, a condition where product price is determined along an extremely well-specified, easily measurable, and easily comparable dimension. Once a product is commoditized, companies have no choice but to drive down cost.

Commoditization drives corporate consolidation, as seen in the Hewlett-Packard merger with Compaq Computer in 2002. But there are clear limits to the benefits of cost competition through merger. Maintaining profits amid cost competition in a commoditized product sector is extremely difficult. Most players are bleeding red ink in the commoditized PC industry.

Examples of Differentiation

Companies can differentiate their offerings in different ways when the market is at a stage where there is still room to differentiate along specified value dimensions.

Matsushita Electric Industrial scored a remarkable success with its DIGA Series DVD recorder, securing a 45% share of the worldwide market in 2003 by being the industry front-runner in terms of miniaturization and advanced functionality. Matsushita has dramatically shrunk printed circuit board size with each new DVD recorder model; its fourth-generation product is one-sixth the size of its first. Meanwhile, models featuring a progressive playback function that displays high-resolution images have been a hit time and again (*Nikkei Business* 2003a).

Casio Computer's first digital camera, the QV-10, was a groundbreaking product that could easily be considered the dominant design driving the full-scale launch of Japan's digicam market. At the time the QV-10 was released, manufacturers featured pixel count as the key value dimension. Sony, Canon, Olympus Optical, Fuji Film, and Matsushita jumped into the market, and Casio's share quickly diminished as rivals competed on the basis of high image resolution as defined by pixel count. In response, Casio adopted a strategy of intense focus on product thinness and compact size. A goal of producing a camera the size of a business card and only 10 millimeters (mm) thick was set. It held pixel count to 1.3 million and eliminated a zoom feature (*Nikkei Business* 2003b).

Facing Commoditization

In sectors that still have room for dimensional innovation, dimensional differentiation can increase WTP. Sooner or later, though, it reaches its limits, and market players face the threat of commoditization. In fact, in the competition for ever smaller, lighter, thinner models, Matsushita released a digital camera that is not just 9.9 mm thick, but also features a music playback function.

The problem is one of customer perception of limits rather than strict technological boundaries. At some point, users stop paying the prices that justify the investment needed for further technological innovation.

Companies operating in a commoditized environment face a difficult choice: accepting commoditization and striving to further reduce costs, or escaping commoditization by creating new, nonprice value and increasing WTP. The first choice is one few companies can make. In the PC industry, Dell is the only company generating significant earnings. Under cost-based competition, there can only be one—or at best an extremely limited number—of winners. Accordingly, most companies faced with commoditization must choose another path: decommoditizing by increasing WTP.

Thus, from the perspective of value-dimension visibility, commoditization can be understood as the phenomenon whereby product or service value converges along the simple dimension of price, after competing firms are unable to differentiate themselves along traditional value dimensions due to the limitations of either technology or customer cognition. Once commoditization is perceived in this way, a certain strategic direction emerges by which a company might boost WTP and escape the commoditization trap.

A Strategy for Decommoditization

Nondimensional differentiation, which seeks to create WTP in the product's external context where the customer and the product interact, is a strategy for decommoditization. Such a strategy disrupts the very rules of dimensional competition. It seeks to transform competition on a basis of invisible dimensions of values. Therefore, it might be called a dimension-breaking strategy. The basic concept of this strategy is that *because high value-dimension visibility invokes commoditization, commoditization can be avoided if value dimensions are rendered invisible.*

A nondimensional differentiation strategy seeks opportunities to improve WTP in the context of customers benefiting from using the product or service. Nondimensional differentiation has two basic directions: consultation and concept innovation. The next two sections explore these.

Consultation: Seeing the Invisible Dimension

Consultation is the process of getting into a customer's inner workings and independently perceiving value dimensions other companies cannot see. It is a strategy of seeing the invisible dimension that is difficult for rivals to see. IBM, Keyence, and Weathernews are examples of companies overcoming commoditization by achieving nondimensional differentiation based on consultation.

Buffeted by the twin trends toward downsizing and customer preference for open systems, IBM (including IBM Japan) was rapidly losing WTP. It recovered by shifting strategy to providing solutions rather than selling hardware or software per se. The essence of IBM's differentiation lies in the process of matching specific ways of using systems with individual customers. The added value is created when IBM shows a particular customer a new, optimal way of using a system by assembling elements into an "on demand" solution.

IBM's move to a solutions business can be understood as a major strategic shift away from dimensional hardware- and software-based differentiation, and to a nondimensional solution-based differentiation. IBM's knowledge and expertise as to what kind of IT system should be installed to solve customer problems, and how that system should be used, is the solution value's core. The solution's value has no highly visible dimensions of the kind seen in mere hardware and software. A "good solution" is specific to a customer, rather than a measurable value the entire industry can share.

By developing products that production-line workers and R&D staff instinctively want to buy, Keyence, the leading sensor and measuring equipment manufacturer in Japan, has managed to achieve average annual operating income levels of more than 40% since 2000. This comes from its salespeople being able to penetrate deep into production and R&D environments and focus on discovering solutions even customer employees fail to perceive.

For example, one of Keyence's most profitable products is its BL Series of bar code readers, designed specifically for use on manufacturing lines. The bar code industry was well developed by the 1980s, following technological advances as bar codes were increasingly used to manage products in transport, distribution, and manufacturing settings. With the BL Series, Keyence shifted strategy to create a device dedicated specifically to production lines. Customers did not give Keyence concrete product specifications; they merely expressed vague desires to somehow "make inventory management a little more efficient at the shop-floor level."

The innovation came in the customer value Keyence created by uncovering latent needs on factory floors and accomplishing production and R&D efficiency improvements. Keyence has 50,000 customers, mostly small and medium enterprises. Customers readily buy its bar code readers in spite of their price, because Keyence provides useful products that on-the-ground manufacturing and research workers at smaller firms instinctively want to buy. This enables Keyence to maintain profitability without being drawn into price competition (*Nikkei Business* 2003c).

Both the IBM and Keyence stories are examples of shifting from products to solutions and services, a notion that has become a commonplace in the last few years. But the fundamental change actually was that the product and service value dimensions became invisible.

Weathernews is the world's largest weather information company, with annual revenues of ¥12 billion. It has 19 stations worldwide that gather data and analyze and forecast weather trends. Basic meteorological data is almost a commodity. What makes Weathernews the world leader is its risk communication service, a form of consultation based on weather data. Weathernews does more than merely forecast the weather; it processes and delivers information in packages designed to fit the specific needs of many clients worldwide who have strong needs to know about the weather. Such customers include convenience stores, whose sales volumes and supply orders change with the weather, and power companies, whose supplies fluctuate due to lightning.

Weathernews offers a comprehensive disaster prevention service that suggests how customers such as governments and farming communities should prepare and respond to earthquakes, typhoons, or other severe weather. More than 1,500 clients use its risk communication service. And a growing number of individual consumers are paying to receive the service via NTT DoCoMo's i-mode mobile telephones.

Consultation versus Customizing

On the face of it, consultation may seem nothing more than the process of identifying values: in other words, customization. Customizing by identifying individual values is an outside-in approach whereby the provider furnishes products and services matched to specific customer needs. In this sense, it is similar to consultation. But the two processes are, in fact, very different.

Customization is based on the premise that the customer already knows what value is needed, and can express it in dimensional terms. Consultation involves discovery on behalf of customers stuck in situations where they cannot grasp or express their needs in dimensional terms. In this sense, consultation is a strategy that seeks to add value by seeing the invisible.

For example, makers of the small liquid crystal display (LCD) screens used in mobile handsets offer high-level customization services in response to handset maker demands. One handset may require a large display with faithful color reproduction, while another may require a smaller display with high contrast. Because of this, LCD manufacturers must produce separate, individual screens with different combinations of size and functionality. With this kind of customization, customers define beforehand the exact LCD specifications they require.

Consultation, in comparison, means customer needs are not broken into clear value dimensions beforehand. That's precisely where the value of consultation lies. Under customization, all that remains is to compete in terms of cost performance along the lines of predefined value dimensions: nondimensional differentiation is impossible. Customization means reactively accepting clear customer needs; consultation means proactively identifying unclear needs.

Concept Innovation: Showing the Invisible Dimension

The nondimensional differentiation strategy can take another form: concept innovation. "Concept" is used here as a compressed representation of an essential customer value: what the product or service means to a customer, what it is used for, and why it is valuable. (See Kusunoki 2004 for a detailed discussion of product concept innovation.)

Dimensional differentiation seeks to differentiate products and services along specific measures such as function or quality. In contrast, while concept innovation encompasses multiple latent values, it does not match these one by one with existing value dimensions. Instead, it paints an entirely new picture of how, why, and to whom a product or service should appeal.

Sony's Walkman, introduced in 1979, is a classic example of new concept creation. Before the Walkman, cassette recorders were seen as music-playing devices, and consumer interest focused on good sound reproduction. In terms of sound quality the Walkman was actually inferior to rival cassette tape players and lacked recording capability. But these became nonissues. Dramatically smaller and lighter than other cassette players, the essence of the Walkman's value lay in its newly created concept of "freedom to enjoy music anywhere." This shows how the essence of nondimensional differentiation lies in *disrupting existing value dimensions and rendering rankings along conventional scales meaningless.*

Although the home-use game industry may be characterized by relatively low value-dimension visibility, it is fair to say that Sony's strategy in this field has been to compete primarily using dimensional differentiation. Sony's PlayStation 2 (PS2), the product that dramatically expanded the company's market share, overwhelmed competitive machines in terms of image quality, complex motion, and video smoothness.

PS2 innovated on easily understandable value dimensions such as polygon count and audio quality. Sony is continuing down this path with its next-generation game player using the new Cell chip developed by Sony, Toshiba, and IBM. Sony says the chip, which has nine processors, is about 60 times faster for graphics than the chip in the PS2.

Pursuing this type of dimensional value requires game software makers to invest time and money in building ever-more sophisticated graphics into their products. Because software scale and complexity have grown so dramatically, only a handful of the biggest houses can afford the necessary development resources.

From a consumer standpoint, increasing sophistication means players must invest considerable effort and practice in learning to play. This has driven many away. Japan's home-use game market peaked in 1997. In particular, the percentage of elementary school students playing with game machines is dwindling. These consumer interests are reportedly drifting away from complex, high-priced game software toward card games, *beigoma* tops, and other, easier-to-enjoy toys (*Asahi Shimbun*, February 29, 2004).

Amid this maturing market, Nintendo—in stark contrast to Sony—shifted away from traditional feature-centric dimensional competition and adopted a strategy of nondimensional differentiation. Judging that consumers were already well-satisfied with current game functionality, in 2004, Nintendo decided not to release a successor to its GameCube line. Its strategy was to go back to creating fun through nondimensional toys. It did this by focusing on accessible, easy-to-play, yet absorbing, laugh-out-loud games with mass appeal, such as Mario and Pokemon. (*Nihon Keizai Shimbun*, February 10, 2004.)

Because it internally does not develop or manufacture high-performance semiconductors or other key game-player components, Nintendo was constrained in its capabilities to drive game-console competition through technological expertise, as Sony has. But even before extreme functionality-driven console competition began, Nintendo had a tradition of seeking competitive superiority by developing software such as Pokemon that appeals to a broad and deep customer segment centered on children.

An explosive, worldwide hit, Pokemon began life in 1986 running on an eight-bit machine that was outdated at the time. One of the key factors in its success was Nintendo putting the game's nondimensional "fun" front and center by deliberately selecting a low-priced game console with abbreviated functionality. Nintendo employed an electronic format to enable players to enjoy collecting and trading 151 different types of Pokemon cards with their friends, but that fun didn't depend on imaging processing or sound-effect technologies. Amid a maturing game market, Sony's strategic intent of dimensional differentiation and Nintendo's choice to disregard existing game rules and differentiate along invisible dimensions offer good examples of contrasting strategies.

Function and Value

The crux of the difference between dimensional innovation and concept innovation may be easier to understand in terms of the relationship between function and value. Function is a value a corporation can predefine in dimensional terms. It comprises only a portion of the value a product or service provides, but when value dimensional visibility is high, improving a particular function nearly always translates directly into better value. Consider PCs: faster speed, bigger memory, and larger storage capacity translates as-is into higher value. In short, under dimensional innovation, the relationship between function and value is clear and easy to understand.

Under concept innovation, however, there is a huge gap between function and value, and the relationship between the two becomes unclear. This can be illustrated with a hardware example: the *pachinko* machine, a Japanese form of pinball. *Pachinko* machine maker Sammy consistently posts strong earnings by developing new-concept products. Value lies in the leisure-time enjoyment provided a player. Yet, while a *pachinko* machine's functionality can be described along various dimensions, the cause and effect relationship between particular combinations of functionality— and the enjoyment each produces—is extremely unclear. Functionality explains only a tiny portion of the value produced through concept innovation.

Consider a service sector example. Secom, which created the concept of "home security" in Japan, enjoys more than an 80% market share. Home security's value lies in safety and peace of mind. Secom has innovated dimensionally by developing highly efficient, low-error, emergency-detecting sensors and other service and product features, but the functionality these provide is not what enabled the company to overwhelm competitors. Peace of mind is hardly a value that can be reduced to or explained by functionality.

It is easy to demonstrate to customers the value of specific differentiated functionality. But it is no trivial matter to get customers to understand the value of nondimensionally differentiated services or products, precisely because the value dimensions are invisible. The key to concept innovation is making customers understand the invisible value of concept innovation. Thus, concept innovation is an approach of showing customers the invisible dimension.

Nondimensional differentiation driven by concept innovation is also superior to dimensional differentiation in terms of sustainability. Once a company succeeds in establishing a new product or service concept, it is often able to produce powerful loyalty and brand effects that trump dimensional superiority.

One of the strengths of nondimensional differentiation is that customers find comparisons difficult. Brands based on dimensional differentiation are relatively easily damaged when rivals successfully overtake them along dimensional competitive metrics. But once a company succeeds in creating new customer value at a conceptual level, it becomes difficult for customers to compare competitive products. That makes it easier to maintain differentiation over the long term. For example, it was relatively easy to replicate and even improve on the Walkman's hardware functionality and quality, as a number of companies did. However, concept-creating products have already defined what is better. Thus, Sony maintained the Walkman brand for a long time, and customers continued to recognize it as different from rivals.

Implications for Knowledge Management

Nondimensional differentiation strategy and its power for decommoditization have important implications for the disciplines of creating and managing knowledge. Context-dependent tacit knowledge is important for nondimensional differentiation. Nondimensional differentiation focuses on the context in which customers derive value from products and services. Under dimensional differentiation, customer-product interaction is a relatively minor issue.

Value can be context-independently defined and perceived. However, under nondimensional differentiation, the interaction between product and customer is crucial. This is because both the consultation and concept innovation approaches require adding new value and getting customers to recognize it. The key is producing tacit knowledge—in the context of product-customer interactions.

According to the SECI (socializing, externalizing, combining, internalizing) model, knowledge is created through four recurring processes. Externalizing means codifying tacit knowledge. Combining means assembling codified chunks to put in SECI order. Internalizing means making codified knowledge tacit. Socializing means adopting others' tacit knowledge as one's own. Internalization and socialization are particularly important for deepening tacit knowledge, and the key issue becomes the context (place, *ba*) in which knowledge interactions take place.

Know-How versus Know-What

In conventional competition and differentiation along visible dimensions, *know-how* has been at the core of tacit knowledge that provides a source of advantage. Know-how means expertise in the interdependencies that enable multiple subsystems to function flawlessly as a whole system. To create and accumulate this type of know-how, a company must develop internal contexts within its organization to promote interactions that encourage internalization and socialization. Intel in semiconductors and Toyota in automobiles are typical examples of companies that have built differentiated products by taking advantage of their rich, difficult-to-imitate know-how.

In contrast, the tacit knowledge at the core of the nondimensional differentiation strategy is *know-what.* Know-what views value from the customer's perspective, and involves knowledge of what benefits customers seek and what the product should be like. Successful nondimensional differentiation, whether consultation or concept innovation, depends on the depth and breadth of company know-what.

Thus, the decisive difference between the strategies lies in the difference between producing tacit knowledge in the context of the internal organization and producing it in the external context that encompasses customers.

Market-in versus Product-out

Under the dimensional differentiation paradigm, it may be sufficient for the company to simply secure a channel through which it can talk with customers. This requires understanding what customers are looking for, and what value dimensions and value levels they require, then differentiating accordingly. This is the *market-in* approach.

Under the nondimensional differentiation approach, listening to what customers want is by definition no simple matter, because value-dimension visibility is originally low. After all, customers usually don't have a clear, prior understanding of nondimensional values. Asking customers what they need when they themselves do not know is unlikely to be productive.

There has been a strategic shift from products to solutions since the early 1990s in an attempt to create nondimensional value via consultation. However, if a customer is already aware of dimensional values, the natural thing is to request estimates from multiple solution providers and select the one that satisfies needs at the lowest cost. Despite the "solution" jargon, this approaches perfect commoditization. Nondimensional values are nondimensional precisely because customers do not clearly recognize them beforehand. The "ask" paradigm can actually impede nondimensional differentiation.

The same can be said about concept innovation. When speaking about needs, customers express dissatisfactions and hopes they have had for products up to that point. Their comments are generally predicated along specific value dimensions. Indeed, most large-scale customer research studies present lists of multiple value dimensions deemed important and ask participants to rank them. Even assuming there are latent opportunities to create new product concepts, such efforts to listen to customers inevitably—and ironically—wind up focusing on dimensional differentiation.

Challenges to Knowledge Creation

The nondimensional strategy presents challenging new issues to organizational knowledge creation. Compared to creating an internal context that encourages internalization and socialization, it is far more difficult to create a comparable external context—especially one that encompasses customers over whom a company exerts no direct influence. Companies wanting to implement nondimensional strategies must build bridges to their customers—external contexts for interactions—that allow knowledge to be internalized and socialized more consciously and proactively. Ordinary sales activity, postsales service, market research, and the like are insufficient. Greater depth of customer interaction, both direct and indirect, is indispensable to showing the invisible dimension.

Keyence offers an example of using consulting to successfully create a superb context for interacting with customers. In contrast to rivals, the company sells directly, and more than half of its 1,300 employees are salespeople. Customers describe their needs to Keyence salespeople only in the vaguest of terms. They realize they have factory-floor problems, but they are unable to describe them. Therefore, Keyence salespeople proactively head for production floors. It is common for them to spend hours observing in order to gain insight into customer problems. They bring product demonstration kits, proposals, and the like. They also lend products to customers for several weeks, free of charge, in order to create a powerful context for customer interaction. But it is their ability to see invisible dimensions that makes it possible for Keyence to use consulting to create nondimensional differentiation.

Keyence does not necessarily customize. If the company fully customized its products, the cost could be greater than the increase in WTP. Focusing on individual customers for consultation is totally different from such customization. If a company can build a capability of seeing invisible dimensions, it can be utilized for many consultations with many customers without incurring huge customization cost.

Software development team leaders at Nintendo who have many hit games to their credit do not listen to customers, nor do they spend much time playing games themselves. Instead, their approach is to peer over the shoulders of people playing the games, observing in great detail to discover what users truly seek. The over-the-shoulder perspective allows seeing what users find fun, surprising, and emotionally compelling, or boring and off-putting, and how they move controllers in response to their feelings.

Developers say that frequently moving between the developer and player perspectives is indispensable. For example, while developing Super Mario 64, the Nintendo team believed camera motion would be the key to fun and comfortable three-dimensional play. Until then, in three-dimensional games the camera simply tracked the hero. As a result, the hero often ended up hidden behind an object, invisible to the player.

Showing the Invisible Dimension

The process of getting customers to understand new concept value conceived by the company—showing the invisible dimension—is the most important, yet most difficult, task in concept innovation. Regardless of the fundamental novelty of its concept, once the company has completed a one-time product or service transaction, it can no longer correctly communicate concept values to users. Companies need continuous interactions with users.

Moreover, ongoing customer relationships in the form of conventional after-service and postsale support are inadequate. Follow-up services and postsales support are, on the contrary, activities that guarantee dimensional values such as functionality, performance, and quality. They do not necessarily promote understanding or reinforce nondimensional values. To show the invisible dimension of concept innovation value, companies must deliberately build and provide a context for internalization and socialization.

Spontaneous interactions between customers are the most effective way to communicate nondimensional values embodied in a new product concept. That is, the context for customer interaction is built into the product itself.

Nintendo simultaneously introduced Pokemon in two versions featuring different character ratios. For example, the A-Bok character appears frequently in the "Red" version, while the Persian character is almost entirely absent; in the "Green" version, the ratio is reversed (Shigero 2003). The purpose is to create a mechanism for promoting the nondimensional value of the Pokemon concept, whereby players collect cards, "battle" with friends, and exchange characters. In a sense, a Pokemon game has already begun when potential users look to see which software their friends have, then agonize over whether to buy Red or Green.

In 2004 Nintendo released a new Pokemon series for the Game Boy Advance (GBA), a portable game player. The software is bundled with a wireless adapter which allows GBA owners to transmit data between themselves without incurring communications charges. Previously, GBA owners had to connect by cable to the Internet or other online services to exchange cards or battle friends. The software also has a "Union Room" feature that provides a virtual space in which wireless adapter-equipped GBA users can assemble. On entering the Union Room, the player's wireless adapter automatically searches for other comparably equipped players in the area, and starts transmitting when it finds one.

These initiatives can be understood as Nintendo's way of promoting customer understanding of the nondimensional value inherent in the product concept by furnishing a context for spontaneous user interactions.

Conclusion

This chapter has looked at the electronics industry as context to discuss competition, innovation, and differentiation from the viewpoint of value-dimension visibility. Amid ongoing commoditization, companies must devise strategies for regaining customer WTP. The nondimensional differentiation strategy sheds light on issues often overlooked under conventional theories that assume the existence of clear competitive dimensions. Escaping commoditization through nondimensional differentiation requires reconceptualizing competition and differentiation under a completely different paradigm. That is the key message of this chapter.

Nondimensional differentiation and value-dimension visibility are not entirely new concepts. Companies in the fashion and entertainment industries have long been acutely aware of these ideas. Strategy, marketing, and innovation scholars, too, have discussed related issues, if only in bits and pieces, using terms such as value proposition, solution strategy, mass customization, experience economy, emotional benefits, brand, consumer relationship management, design management, and so forth.

One key benefit of the value-dimension visibility perspective is its potential to provide a common language for the many arguments and experiences expounded in different industries and functional sectors. In so doing, these concepts might provide a logical base for linking disparate arguments.

Most companies are only vaguely aware of the nondimensional differentiation strategy. Even those who adopt it tend to do so only in a superficial manner, changing product sensibility, adopting a new design sense, or implementing a shift to services. Japan's latent nondimensional competitive abilities have attracted much attention in the new millennium. As the expression "cool Japan" indicates, these abilities are highly regarded overseas. In home electronics, in particular, ever since the Walkman was released, the type of concept innovation discussed here has played a critical role in building Japanese corporate competitiveness. At the very least, proximity to a Japanese market with tens of millions of customers willing to enjoy "fun products" is an extremely valuable asset for the nation's corporations.

The arguments of nondimensional differentiation include important implications for businesses in developing countries. Given the conventional assumptions of dimensional competition, it would take a painstakingly long time for them to catch up with developed countries in order to increase WTP, because creating differentiation along visible dimensions usually require substantial accumulation of technological capabilities in the internal context of a company.

The nondimensional differentiation, however, depends more on external contexts in which products or services are used by customers, whereas the dimensional differentiation is relatively independent of external contexts on the customer side. Therefore, businesses in developing countries have had to concentrate on reducing costs rather than increasing WTP, taking advantage of less costly human and other resources available in their home countries.

Considering the nature of nondimensional competition, one can assume that companies in developing countries are in a better position to see and show invisible value dimension to customers in their unique, domestic markets. Just as Sony and other Japanese companies have done with unique customers in Japan, electronics companies in developing countries face great opportunities to create unique concepts though interacting with customers in their home markets.

References

Fortune. 2002, October 28. "The PC's New Tricks."

Fortune. 2003, September 15. "Video Game Planet."

Kusunoki, Ken. 2004, "Value Differentiation: Organizing Know-What for Product Concept Innovation." In Takeuchi and Nonaka, editors, *Hitotsubashi on Knowledge Management.* Singapore: John Wiley & Sons (Asia).

Nikkei Business. 2003a, July 14. "Kita zo, Digital AV Keiki [Good Times are Here for Digital AV]."

Nikkei Business. 2003b, June 23. "Casio no Gyakutenuchi Keiei [Casio's Comeback Management]."

Nikkei Business. 2003c, October 27. "Keyence no Himitsu [Keyence's Secret]."

Shigero, Nihara. 2003. *Nihon no Yushu Kigyou Kenkyu (Inquiries into Outstanding Japanese Companies).* Nihon Keizai Shimbunsha.

6

Interorganizational Knowledge Creation at Shimano

Hirotaka Takeuchi

The knowledge creation process applies equally well *across* organizational boundaries as *within* an organization, and there is a "knowledge ecosystem" that extends beyond the organization. Earlier analysis of knowledge creation has focused primarily on what happens within an organization. In particular, although Nonaka and Takeuchi recognize the importance of interorganizational knowledge creation in their 1995 book *The Knowledge-Creating Company*, the task of explaining how to create conditions for knowledge creation outside a firm's boundaries was left to future research (Ahmadjian 2004, p. 229). This is a step toward completing that task.

In particular, the chapter examines how Shimano Inc., the leading parts manufacturer in the world for high-end bicycles and mountain bikes, works with its outside constituents to create interorganizational knowledge.

Japanese companies have continually turned to their suppliers, customers, dealers, local communities, and even competitors for new insights and clues. Knowledge acquired from the outside is shared widely within the company, stored as part of the company's knowledge base, and utilized by those engaged in developing new technologies, products, systems, or ways of competing.

Toyota Motor Corp. is the classic example of a company that works closely with a group of affiliated suppliers to create knowledge across organizational boundaries. Toyota suppliers not only share knowledge with Toyota, they also are required to share knowledge with other suppliers (Ahmadjian 2004, p. 231). Toyota's process of interorganizational knowledge creation moves through the four modes of knowledge conversion (the SECI process described by Nonaka and Takeuchi 1995) in a spiraling manner. Tacit knowledge, created by Toyota and its suppliers through social interactions, is made explicit, combined with knowledge across Toyota's network of suppliers, and internalized within the group.

What sets Shimano apart from other case studies is fourfold. They can be summarized with a hub-and-spoke analogy. Shimano sits at the "hub" of a large number of "spokes." Knowledge exchange occurs across the spokes. The spokes are global, and the hub involves a cluster. A closer look at each of these follows.

First, it has a large number of outside constituents with which it forms a knowledge ecosystem. As discussed later, an ecosytem is composed of *ba* (a network for knowledge exchange; in Japanese, it is written with the character meaning "place"). As such, a knowledge ecoysystem is the broad context in which knowledge is shared, created, and utilized through interactions that occur in a specific time and space. Included in Shimano's ecosystem are bicycle manufacturers, dealers, bicycle users, professional racers, universities, competitors, and the local community. (The concepts of *ba* and knowledge ecosystem are developed more fully later.)

Second, knowledge exchange occurs across outside constituents, as well as between Shimano and its outside constituents. The knowledge that is acquired from professional racers, for example, is shared with bicycle manufacturers and dealers in developing new products and technologies.

Third, the unique feature of Shimano's interorganizational knowledge creation process—both *between* the hub and spokes, as well as *across* the spokes—is the broad geographic spread of the *ba*. In high-end road bikes, the knowledge exchange is between Shimano and its dealers, and it takes place primarily in the United States. In mountain bikes, the exchange is between Shimano and its core users, and it takes place in the United States. Finally, there is an exchange between Shimano and professional racers, which takes place in Europe.

Fourth, the Shimano case provides a rare example of a cluster model at work in Japan.[1] Sakai, the city where Shimano originated, forms an industry "cluster" for bicycle parts. Although Japanese companies have been exemplars of interorganizational knowledge creation along the lines of the Toyota model, Japanese companies are generally perceived to have had less success replicating a cluster model (see, for example, Ahmadjian 2004).

The chapter is organized as follows. After an overview of Shimano and its history, the chapter examines how Shimano has incorporated each of the features of the Japanese approach to knowledge outlined in chapter 1. There is special focus on the utilization of knowledge created by outside constituents to amplify the knowledge spiral.

1. A cluster consists of industries and firms that form vertical (suppliers, channels, and buyers) or horizontal (common skills, technology, or inputs) relationships in geographically concentrated groups (Ishikura 2004, p. 185). Silicon Valley and Hollywood are examples of clusters.

Shimano: Background

Shimano is the dominant supplier of parts for high-end bikes. Today, 90% of bikes sold by the top three brands in the United States—Trek, Giant, and Specialized—use some Shimano parts. Shimano parts set the standard for the industry in quality and innovation. As a result, it is much more profitable than its competitors. Its five-year (1998–2002) weighted average gross margin (ROS) was 14.6%, and its return on invested capital (ROIC) was 16.6%. This compares to 1.2% ROS and 4.2% ROIC for international competitors and 0.3% ROS and 0.3% ROIC for domestic competitors.

Shimano has consistently led the market with new developments. In mountain bikes (MTBs), the company pioneered development of rugged, shock-absorbing derailleurs designed for offroad use in the 1980s. It now commands an over-80% global market share in MTBs. Other developments include pedals that riders can click into like a ski binding (Dura-Ace with Shimano Index System [SIS]) and gearshifts built into brake levers (Dura-Ace with Shimano Total Integration [STI]). STI became the de facto industry standard because it made riding easier for riders and assembling and adjusting easier for bike assemblers and dealers. Today, Shimano is developing a new line of computer-controlled shifting and suspension systems for shopping and commuting bikes.

In the racing world, it took over a decade, beginning in the mid-1980s, for Shimano to be accepted by top racers. In the 1996 Atlanta Olympics, the 12 top finishers in the men's racing event rode a bike with Shimano pedals, cranks, derailleurs, and brakes. Over two-thirds of the teams participating in the Tour de France now utilize Shimano components. Lance Armstrong won the Tour seven years in a row (1999 to 2005) riding a bike powered by Shimano's Dura-Ace system. (Dura stands for duralumin, an aluminum alloy, and durability. Ace invokes Shimano's commitment to standards of world-class excellence.)

The company also manufactures fishing rods and reels, and snowboard boots and bindings. Bicycle components, however, accounted for 75% of Shimano's $1.5 billion in revenues and 80% of its profits in 2004. Shimano products are sold predominantly outside Japan (84%), with Europe accounting for 40%, other Asia 26%, the Americas 17%. Bikes are manufactured in 14 factories in nine countries.

Company History

Shimano Inc. was founded as an iron foundry in 1921 in Sakai, which had become Japan's center for bicycle manufacturing. There were 60 companies in 1919, and 106 by 1921, many of which had only four or five employees. Competition was fierce.

Shozaburo Shimano, 26 at the time, started the company with a colleague from his apprentice days. Shozaburo had apprenticed as a cutler when he was 15 and later worked for a company making bicycle chain wheels, as well as for Sakai Bicycle, one of the larger bicycle manufacturers at that time. The newly established company produced freewheels, the core of the driving gear of a bicycle.

Shozaburo died in 1958, and each of his three sons succeeded, in turn, to the presidency. Each took a different route to the top. Also, the two youngest followed the custom in many family-owned businesses in Japan of the children of the owners spending some time at other firms—mostly larger firms in related industries—as a training process.

The eldest, Shozo, joined the company at 18 and worked in sales and production before taking over as president at age 30. Keizo, the second son, studied engineering at Keio University and worked for Fujikoshi, a specialized steel manufacturer, before joining Shimano, where he worked primarily in R&D. Yoshizo, the third son, studied economics at Keio University and worked for carmaker Nissan before joining Shimano, where he was responsible for international operations. Insiders say each brought a very different temperament and personality to the company, but they functioned well as a team. The surviving brother, Yoshizo, is chairman. Shozo's son Yozo serves as the fifth president.

Note that the name of each son ends in *zo*. This is a reading of the character for three, which can also be read *sabu*, as in their father's name. This may be the reason Shozaburo started to use the trademark "3-3-3" for his freewheels in 1922.

The Company Viewed as a Living Organism

Shuzo Matsumoto joined Shimano in 1954 with a dream. A graduate of the Electrical Engineering Department of Osaka Prefecture University, he saw his mission as introducing cold-forging technology to replace the hot-forging techniques then used. To achieve this goal, he was dispatched to the United States and Europe for two and a half months. Meeting company president Shozaburo right before his departure, he was told simply, "Enjoy the trip." Matsumoto recalled the incident as follows:

> In those days, there was a limit on the amount of foreign currency that could be taken out of Japan. It was too small an amount to live on. So, he gave me a lot of dollars obtained from the black market. You cannot believe it today! He gave me dollars and told me to enjoy the trip. . . . That was the kind of company it was. What an interesting and exciting company. (Shimano Inc. 2004, pp. 18–19)

Entrusting a new employee with an important mission eventually led Shimano to adopt cold forging in the late 1950s, ahead of all other companies in Japan, including Toyota. Matsumoto was thus the "knowledge engineer" behind introduction of a technology that re-created the entire company. Although told to enjoy the trip, Matsumoto had a shared understanding of the company mission. (The details of the trip are discussed later.)

Knowledge begins with an individual, but the interaction between the individual and the company plays an important role in creating organizational knowledge.

The pursuit of dreams and ideals is the mission every worker is expected to strive for within Shimano. The company's mission statement clearly demonstrates how the company views itself—as a living organism, not a machine:

In close relationship with nature
To set people's hearts full and free
To realize the new dream
To promote health and happiness
We will continue to create products
that excite the heart of people.

This statement illustrates that a company can have a collective sense of identity and fundamental purpose, much like an individual.

Knowledge as Justified Belief

Knowledge has been passed down at Shimano for three generations in the form of beliefs that are deeply rooted in personal values. "Quality, technology, and credibility" was the credo of Shozaburo, the founder. The three sons heard these words countless times, and never forgot them. This credo was the foundation on which the Shimano business was built and nurtured. Thus, Shozo, who succeeded his father, put forth three guidelines when he was president.

1. Put your whole soul into the product. The product represents your personality.
2. Do not try to sell the product. Sell yourself.
3. Put yourself in the other person's position. That gives you a broader perspective.

These guidelines are beliefs that emerge out of Shozo's subjective view of the world. They represent a call for human action, which is what knowledge is all about.

Keizo, the third president, used the phrase "look good, handle good, and ride good." In this regard, he often noted that the criteria and standards determining what he meant in practice could change completely. His philosophy was to start from casting doubt on an existing product, as reflected in the following.

> Bicycles and their components are not friendly to users even now. Manufacturers are not able to offer user-friendly tools for consumers. When the manufacturers realize the need for improvements in their products, it would become a business opportunity. We are able to take advantage of our capacity to resolve inconveniences that consumers currently suffer from. (Shimano Inc. 2004, p. 57)

This personal belief of Keizo's still constitutes a key pillar of the corporate philosophy.

Yoshizo, who later became the fourth president, established Shimano American Corporation (SAC) in 1965. The prevalent view of Japanese products at the time was "cheap and shoddy," so Shimano had a hard time convincing people to even try its products. That experience cultivated a belief in Yoshizo that "you have to create demand if you want to sell." He also observed firsthand that Americans enjoy riding bicycles in the same way they enjoy playing with toys, which led to another belief of his: "offer products with *play value.*"

Yoshizo's 27 years in the United States (1965–92) led to his belief that English had become the de facto standard in business communications. As a result, English was adopted as the official language within Shimano in 1997. "After adopting English as an official language, non-Japanese-speaking staff members began contributing with greater enthusiasm," Yoshizo noted. In a July 2005 interview, he noted that "Domestic employees were perplexed and rattled at the outset. . . . Hundreds of workers started taking English conversation lessons. If they reached a certain level, the company paid the lesson fees. If not, they had to pay for the lessons on their own. . . . Some 200 executives from 21 different countries came together for our biannual planning meeting last month. During the entire week, all conversations and documents were in English."

Emphasis on Tacit Knowledge

Being an engineer, Keizo often spoke of the three fundamental principles that engineers should obey: basic, general, and onsite. Basic refers to concepts, general relates to the laws of physics, and onsite refers to firsthand experience. Onsite was what Keizo regarded as most important. He showered people around him with such questions as "Did you ride the bicycle?" or "Did you see it with your own eyes?"

On the advice of Keizo, a newly hired engineer named Takashi Segawa started riding a bicycle to and from work. He gradually came to understand the strengths and weaknesses of the bicycle he was riding. Inspired by his own experience, he was able to design specific components to improve the performance of his bicycle.

In the mid-1980s, when Keizo and a team of other employees were developing bicycles for women, he ordered his staff to buy skirts. "You can't imagine how the user feels, because your posture on the bicycle is not that of a woman." Keizo rode the bicycle himself, wearing a skirt, in front of a group of hesitant staff members. One staffer also rode in a skirt, but his movements were not natural. "Women don't mount bicycles like that," said Keizo. The staff member was told to bind his legs with an elastic band at the knees and try again. Keizo was still not satisfied. He found fault with the sneakers the staffer was wearing. "You have to wear high-heeled shoes." Someone ran to a shoe shop to buy a pair, and the experiment continued. A new product named the "L-pedal" was commercialized as a result of these experiments.

The onsite principle also came into play with MTBs. Yozo Shimano, the current president, made the final decision to develop MTBs components when he was head of the Sales Planning Division at headquarters. The decision came in 1981 after he and Keizo visited Mount Tamalpais, the birthplace of MTBs. (Tamalpais is north of San Francisco.) What stunned members of the U.S. subsidiary was Yozo riding down the rugged, slippery trails, his suit trousers completely stained with mud. He gave his go-ahead saying, "What we need is to incorporate mud- and water-free function and strength" (Shimano Inc. 2004, p. 155).

As these anecdotes indicate, Shimano is a living example of a company that recognizes the value of learning from the direct experience of trial and error. Yozo's 25 years living in the United States gave the company valuable insights on what features were being demanded by Americans.

The same thing happened in Europe in the early 1970s when Hiroshi Nakamura was dispatched from headquarters to be the first Japanese to join a professional racing team in Europe. What he saw shocked him: extensive damage that never occurred under normal test conditions. He reported the details and other relevant information (such as climatic and road conditions, assessment of competing brands, detailed work performed by mechanics, and the like) to the development team in Japan. Each report was passed around to every Dura-Ace team staff member. Everyone understood that the barrier to entering Europe was higher than expected. More important, as a result of Nakamura's contribution, Shimano was on the verge of grasping the essence of bicycle racing.

These examples vividly illustrate the SECI process. Nakamura's travel with professional racers in Europe is socialization. Putting down what he experienced into reports is externalization. Circularizing the reports within headquarters is combination. The outcome, a higher-order understanding of the essence of bicycle racing, is internalization.

The Central Role of Self-Organizing Teams

Shimano has always worked as a team when developing something new. This has been the case whether developing a product, a geographic market, or a customer segment. In the early days, there may have been no choice. In the mid-1960s, the headquarters was on one floor. Everyone in the company, including Shozo, the president, was in a single large room. Young staff members could be seen assembling test parts onto bicycles beside directors making international calls. This constituted an ideal *ba* for information exchange and team formation, as discussed further later.

Shimano still works as a team, even though its factories are located in nine countries and non-Japanese local hires account for 85% of its global work force of 6,500. In the early 1990s, Keizo, as president, introduced the "Team Shimano" principle to respond proactively to globalization of the workforce. His rationale was the following.

> If a company has more overseas factories, there is the possibility that it can produce the same product in multiple factories. In such a case, the quality of a product might vary from place to place unless they share the same knowledge, wisdom, and technology. To prevent this from occurring, the headquarters and subsidiaries have to be united as one to develop new technologies and to establish and strengthen the world-wide sales network. All will compete with each other in terms of technologies and aim at cost reduction. (Shimano Inc. 2004, p. 180)

Keizo realized that it was essential to unite the international work force with common principles, a common system of operational process management, and a common language. His aim was to establish a working environment imbued with mutual trust and the spirit of teamwork by binding staff members representing different cultural backgrounds from around the world under the principle of "Team Shimano."

The Importance of Middle Managers

Throughout its history, Shimano has relied heavily on middle managers to lead important projects. It was the pioneering efforts of middle managers that enabled Shimano to establish a foothold in the U.S. market, make inroads into the European market, and develop breakthrough products. The next sections illustrate the important role of middle managers in relation to three key events in Shimano's growth.

All the middle managers mentioned served as the bridge between top management and frontline workers in a process described in chapter 1 as the middle-up-down management process. They all understood what top management had in mind regarding where the company should be headed ("what ought to be"), as well as what frontline workers faced in reality ("what is"). Middle managers at Shimano resolved the contradiction between what top management hoped to create and what actually existed in the real world by creating mid-range concepts.

Establishing a U.S. Presence

Middle managers from headquarters led the effort to make inroads into the U.S. market. Thus, in 1971, three teams were assigned to conduct a sales promotion tour.

Each team consisted of two experienced middle managers uprooted from important positions at headquarters. Travelling in a station wagon, with brochures and service parts packed in the back, each team visited retail bicycle shops throughout the country to teach shop owners and staff how to maintain and repair Shimano products.

Team members received no special training in either presentation or language skills. They were instructed simply to "go." Within its region, each team visited one town after another, looking for shops at which it could engage in promotion activities. "Show and tell" was used to supplement presentations in English. Whatever the members lacked in presentation and English-language skills, they more than made up for with plenty of tacit knowledge (based on experience, five senses, emotions, feelings, conviction, beliefs, and so on). They spoke from their hands (technical experience) and their hearts. That is why they were able to bond with bicycle shop owners and workers.

The teams travelled for six months. By Shimano's account, the tour, termed a "caravan" in the company's history, was a huge success. The method has been repeated continuously as one of the best means of listening to the voice of retailers and communicating with them.

Entering Europe

In 1972, Osamu Takaoka, then 32, was asked by President Shozo to "go to Europe and eventually get married there." Takaoka had been in the United States for six years when Shozo approached him. "If you get married in a distant place, you will not be able to come back to your hometown very often. I meant that you should adjust to a life in Europe and do your best there," explained Shozo (Shimano Inc. 2004, p. 71).

Takaoka knew how important Europe was to the company but realized, after spending some time there, that Europe would be a tougher market for an unknown manufacturer from Japan to enter than the United States had been. Takaoka realized many Europeans used bicycles differently than Americans. As in the United States, most people in Germany, the Netherlands, and Scandinavia considered a bicycle a vehicle for children and a means for adults to get around town. In contrast, the French used bicycles for recreation and Italians equated bicycles with racing machines. Takaoka's insights, communicated to management in Japan, had a strong influence on Shimano's entry strategy into Europe.

In Japan it was Masashi Nagano, a 10-year veteran of the R&D team, who developed a breakthrough innovation called the Positron System in 1974. This was a derailleur equipped with an indexed shifting mechanism. This device allowed the user to move a lever by single-notch shifts to change gears up or down with something akin to a digital sensation. The Positron System also produced a clicking sound every time a shift was made. Because it was a fail-proof system, it was first mounted on sport-type bicycles for children. The mechanism around the shift lever was covered by a box, which looked like the console box of a car gear shift. This touch appealed to children, because gear shifting was identified with driving a car. The clicking sound was also a big hit.

Nagano continued to upgrade the system until it was incorporated into racing components beginning in 1983. Referred to as the SIS, it drastically changed the racing scene, and by 1989–90 had helped establish Shimano as one of the leading manufacturers in Europe.

As a middle manager, Nagano had access to a lot of knowledge, being positioned at the intersection of the vertical and horizontal flows of information in the company. As mentioned in chapter 1, this positioning makes a middle manager an ideal candidate to lead a project team.

Building MTBs

The entry into MTBs in 1982 can be traced to the pioneering efforts of Masaki Sumida, a middle manager who had been with one of the caravans in the United States. He was sent to Shimano Sales Corporation (SSC), which was established in the Los Angeles area as a subsidiary of SAC.

One day, Sumida was taken to the garage of Gary Fisher, known as the father of the MTBs, by a frame builder who made racing bicycles in San Francisco. There, he encountered several bizarre bicycles. One was a BMX (bicycle motocross) with large wheels equipped with a derailleur. Broken parts were scattered all over the place.

As luck would have it, the assistance of an SSC sales representative who belonged to the same racing club as Fisher and Joe Breeze, Sumida became a close acquaintance of Fisher and Breeze. (Breeze is credited with the idea of a MTBs.) Sumida joined their rides. By the end of a day climbing mountains, the bicycles usually had broken down. This meant ongoing repairs and experiments reinforcing their bicycles. Through these experiences, Sumida realized what was needed: gears and derailleurs that could tolerate the harsh conditions, and a braking device that could ensure safety. Sumida sent a prototype to headquarters in order to convert skeptics—many of whom were in top management—into believers. Sumida also accompanied Yozo on the mud-splattered test run down Mount Tamalpais described earlier.

Acquiring Knowledge from Outsiders

After establishing a U.S. sales subsidiary in 1965, Shimano worked closely with leading bicycle manufacturers and retailers in the United States in order to understand the requirements of the market.

Yoshizo Shimano visited Stan Natanek, the head of Schwinn, several times before receiving any order for parts from him. Natanek was called the "Destroyer" within the industry and was known as an expert in finding defects in components. He repeatedly destroyed every component brought to him by Shimano before giving his first stamp of approval. Schwinn was the largest bicycle manufacturer in the United States at the time, but it was the last of the eight U.S. manufacturers to purchase parts from Shimano. (The first was Columbia, which agreed in 1963 to purchase 100,000 three-speed hub gears.)

Yoshizo started visiting the other manufacturers in 1965, but none wanted to do business. Shimano was still unknown to mass merchandisers and the 6,000 U.S. bicycle shops at the time (the caravans began later). Yoshizo realized that bicycle makers would not want to do business with Shimano unless retailers demanded "a bicycle equipped with Shimano parts." Sears, the largest mass merchandiser at the time, was also the largest retailer of bicycles, selling approximately 1 million of the 6 million sold in the United States each year. Sears tested the bicycles they sold using equipment even the manufacturers did not have, and in 1966 it agreed to test Shimano parts. Shimano's three-speed hub gear received high marks for durability and performance, and that eventually led manufacturers to accept Shimano components. Shimano learned U.S. durability and performance requirements from Sears.

Shimano also went out of its way to work closely with bicycle shop owners. Initially, with its caravan, Shimano approached shops to promote its products through "show and tell" sessions. The caravan tradition of visiting shops continues: the company dispatches over a dozen employees each year for three months. However, the purpose is now to acquire knowledge about the needs, wants, habits, or service requirements of end users who visit the shops.

In Europe, working with racers opened the door for Shimano. Nakamura, the employee travelling with the Shimano-sponsored racing team Flandria, recalled what President Keizo told him:

> It's not enough having our components used by the team. We have to know the realities of racing on the ground to improve our products. See who uses the product and how. How are the Shimano products used and how are they damaged? Go and observe with your own eyes what goes on in the racing field. That's the mission. Go to Europe, Nakamura. (Shimano Inc. 2004, p. 85)

Observing racers led to the development of STI in 1988. This breakthrough idea changed Shimano's fortune within the racing world, as well as bicycle racing itself. Previously, the shift lever was on the lower tube of the frame, which meant a racer had to take a hand off the handle bar to shift. To retain stability when ascending, riders sat down while doing this. That meant they could not push down on the pedals with full force, and it caused a few seconds delay. Keizo was confident of success.

> If the shift lever is on the handle bar grip, it can eliminate unnecessary motion. It also helps the rider choose the most appropriate gear. This is a great advantage! (Shimano Inc. 2004, p. 110)

Keizo's confidence was backed by the success with MTBs. Going up and down mountains, MTB users shifted without removing a hand from the handle bar.

STI integrated the brake lever and the shift lever. It was tested in races beginning in 1989 and introduced in 1991 as Dura-Ace 7410. In 1996, it was upgraded as the 7700, which boasted 9 speed gears, and there are now 10.

Other Outside Sources

In addition to working with various members of the "buyer chain"—bicycle manufacturers, large retailers, shop owners, consumers, and racers—Shimano has gained knowledge from three other outsider constituents: universities, competitors, and the local community.

Universities

Universities helped Shimano develop cold-forging technology in the 1950s. Shuzo Matsumoto, told by the founder to enjoy his trip to the United States, also visited Professor Hideaki Kudo at the Technical University of Hanover in Germany. Dr. Otto Kienzle, a world authority on cold forging, showed him a number of cold-forged products. Cold forging has a number of advantages over hot forging. It eliminates deformation caused by heating. As a result, a cutting process is not required to ensure conformity to specifications. This also saves on materials. Moreover, the process is well-suited for mass production, as a single mold can be used many times. The method also permits uniform accuracy.

Matsumoto embarked on developmental research immediately after returning to Japan. But cold forging had never been tried in Japan. So, he relied on two resources. The first was a book in German (*The Flow Forging of Steel* in its English translation), which he read with a German-Japanese dictionary in hand. The second was Professor Hideaki Kudo, the leading Japanese authority on cold forging and a professor at Yokohama National University, as well as director of the Mechanical Engineering Laboratory at the Agency of Industrial Science and Technology. Professor Kudo, who had been in Hanover just before Matsumoto's visit, agreed to work with a consortium of companies interested in the cold-forging technology.

Shimano's relationship with universities goes beyond individual scientists. Besides cold forging, Shimano has built institutional relationships, especially with universities in the Osaka area, in such fields as materials science, mechanical engineering, metallurgy, metal engineering, chemistry, and electronics.

Foreign Competitors

Competitors initially forced Shimano to play catch-up, especially in overseas markets. Italy's Campagnolo reigned as the front-runner in the mid-1950s. At the time, Shimano saw Campagnolo as the "Rolex of the industry" and equated itself to a Seiko. Shimano marveled at the negotiating power Campagnolo had with manufacturers. One Shimano veteran recalls: "It was the bicycle makers who conformed to Campa's components. They listened to new suggestions, like building the shifting lever directly into the frame, coming from Campa. In Japan, we were still subservient to bicycle makers. We made our brake cable to conform to their handle" (Yamaguchi 2003, p. 131).

Even though Shimano's negotiating power vis-à-vis manufacturers improved over time, when Shimano entered the European racing scene in the 1970s a large gap still existed in how racers perceived the two brands. Recalled another veteran: "Even if Campa had the same trouble as our product, it wouldn't be a big deal. But when something went wrong with our product, even if it was a small thing, it became a big problem" (Yamaguchi 2003, p. 197).

Shimano continuously improved its products and relentlessly pursued new ideas in order to catch up with Campagnolo, which may be why the company was once called "a copy of Campa." It undertook a thorough investigation into products made by Campagnolo, even the composition of the metal alloys used.

Conforming to parts made by Campagnolo was a large part of Shimano's success through the 1980s. Industry observers believe Shimano only overtook Campagnolo in 1991, when Dura-Ace 7410 (which had STI) was released. It was a first, with shifters built into brake levers. As a result, Shimano started to win converts in Europe. A member of an Italian team commented that "Everything from the feel of the brakes to shifting speed, Shimano clearly surpassed Campagnolo" (Yamaguchi 2003, p. 54). Shimano also started to win mechanics.

But surpassing Campagnolo on durability was not easy. Campagnolo had a leg up on Shimano when it came to racing under foul conditions. Campagnolo's gears did not wear out as much when it rained. It had better knowledge of how to deal with sand and dirt. Even today, Campagnolo is the company to watch for breakthroughs in racing innovation. For example, Campagnolo is pushing into lighter, carbon-based materials, while Shimano is sticking with aluminum. Carbon is gaining in popularity because it shaves weight, making the bicycle run faster.

Local Community and Competitors

The third outside constituent is Sakai, an industrial city immediately south of Osaka. Capitalizing on its heritage as the center of sword making since the 16th century, the city further flourished as a center of the rifle industry from the 16th century. By 1921, when Shimano was founded, Sakai had established a bicycle "cluster" with 106 small companies. In 1992, the city opened a large bicycle museum to commemorate its heritage as the bicycling center of Japan.

Sakai has a lot of small factories and a large pool of artisans, but the city has been best-known as a city of merchants. In the days of the samurai, it was a rare case of a city in which merchants wielded power, not only financially but also politically. Merchants took advantage of Sakai's location as a port to amass huge fortunes in the wake of the mid-19th century opening to trade with foreign countries. Trade, in turn, exposed the city to foreign culture and language. The penchant for learning from foreign countries was, therefore, strong.

Shimano inherited this tradition, which explains why Shimano has been so progressive in going overseas to learn the latest technology (such as cold forging), to conduct "show and tell" sessions at bicycle shops in small towns (caravans), to join a racing team in Brussels (Team Flandria), or simply to gain a better understanding on how bicycles are used in different countries. It also explains why Shimano made English its official language.

Maeda Industries, once Shimano's biggest domestic competitor, was established in 1922. The two competed on various fronts over the years. In the 1950s, when Shimano was still focused on making a three-speed internal hub gear, Maeda introduced a three-speed external hub gear, which was more suited for sport-oriented bicycles. When Shimano developed an integrated component system (Dura-Ace) in-house, Maeda worked with several other local components manufacturers to develop an integrated system under the Sun Tour brand introduced in 1976. Shimano was forced to undergo a full model change of Dura-Ace as a result of Sun Tour's entry.

Maeda was first to enter the U.S. market, and both companies competed head-on when the MTB boom hit, again with Maeda taking an early lead. Despite the fierce competition in the marketplace, their chief executive officers were friends and met regularly to exchange ideas as well as ideals. Maeda went bankrupt in the mid-1990s.

The Knowledge Ecosystem

The Shimano case shows how important interactions are to creating new knowledge. Interactions take place at a specific time and space both among individuals *within* the company *and* with dealers, consumers, competitors, and others *outside* the company. The context in which knowledge is shared, created, and utilized

Figure 6.1. *Conceptual Representation of* Ba

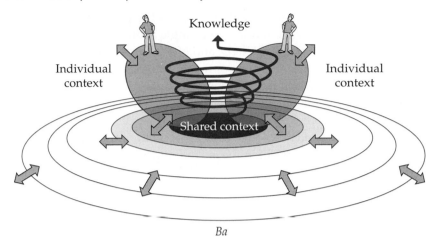

Figure 6.2. *The Knowledge Ecosystem as an Organic Configuration of* Ba: *Case of Shimano*

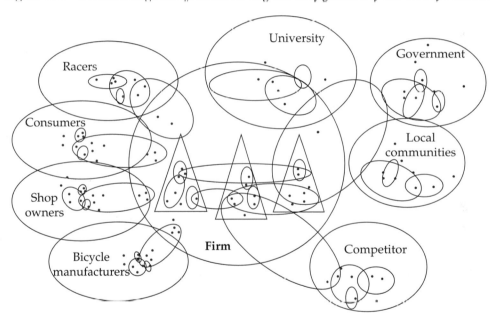

through interactions that occur in a specific time and space is known as a *ba*. Knowledge cannot be created in a vacuum, and needs a place where information is given meaning. Figure 6.1 is a graphical representation of a *ba*.

Figure 6.2 provides a graphical representation of a knowledge ecosystem. Notice that two kinds of *ba* configurations are shown in the figure. The first is the "vertical" *ba*, represented by linkages between members of the buyer chain: the component manufacturer (Shimano), bicycle manufacturers, bicycle shops and retailers, consumers, and professional racers. The second is the "horizontal" *ba*, represented by the linkages between Shimano and universities, competitors, and the local community.

Internal **Ba**

A fitting example of an "internal" *ba* at Shimano is the physical space of its head-quarters in the 1960s. Everyone worked in a single room, including the president; staff in finance, administration, and R&D; and office workers in the production and quality control divisions. Having most of the employees in the same room consti-tuted an ideal context in which interactions could take place.

Another example is the informal meetings held when developing bicycles for women, described earlier. Requiring staff to try to experience bike riding as a woman does—in a skirt and heels—led to development of the L-pedal concept. The interactions took place in a specific time, space, and relationship with others. The meanings and contexts that team members held changed as the experiment moved from one stage to the next. In this sense, a *ba* is a shared context in motion, in which knowledge is shared, created, and utilized.

External **Ba**

What is striking about the knowledge creation process at Shimano is the large num-ber of "external" *ba* it created with outside constituents. Consider, the frontline interactions that took place between Yoshizo Shimano and Schwinn's Stan Natanek, between members of the caravan and bicycle shop owners in the United States, between Nakamura and members of the Flandria Team when they raced in Europe, and between Sumida and Fisher and Breeze when they were riding MTBs on Mount Tamalpais. These interactions took place at a specific time, space, and relationship to others.

In addition to the buyer chain, Shimano created an external *ba* with universities, the local community of Sakai, and even competitors. A lot of knowledge was shared, created, and utilized by building an interactive relationship with these out-side constituents at a specific time, space, and history. Shimano built a knowledge ecosystem, which consists of an organic configuration of various *ba,* where people inside and outside the firm interact with each other and the environment, based on the knowledge they have and the meaning they create.

Special Features of Shimano's Knowledge Ecosystem

In addition to the large number of external participants, two features of Shimano's knowledge ecosystem are striking. The first is the "multilayering" of the various *ba.* The second is its global reach.

Multilayering

An ecosystem is characterized by multilayering. For example, the knowledge acquired from professional racers is shared with consumers and vice versa. Thus, knowledge gained working with Lance Armstrong is utilized in developing faster and more durable high-end road bicycles for enthusiasts. Also, the knowledge gained working with children, who loved the shift lever and its clicking sound, was utilized to develop the SIS and eventually the STI, which professional racers have adopted.

Multilayering takes place not only between two members of the knowledge ecosystem, but also across various members of the vertical buyer chain. For example, the knowledge that Shimano gains from users and shop owners is shared and utilized by bicycle manufacturers in developing new products and technologies.

Global Reach

The second striking feature of the knowledge ecosystem that Shimano has created is its global nature.

Take universities as a case in point. In order to master the cold-forging technology, Shimano not only worked with universities in Japan, including Osaka University and Yokohama National University, but also the Technical University of Hanover in Germany.

The global spread of its competitors is another example. Originally, Shimano faced competitors in the local community of Sakai. Later, the key competitor to watch and learn from was Campagnolo of Italy. Today, Shimano's attention is focused on China, where component makers have popped up to supply mainland manufacturers. Most are still small, but could become formidable competitors if they can boost their quality. To respond to this threat, Shimano is shifting its own production to China.

In 1992, Shimano established a factory in Kunshan, near Shanghai. It began production in 1994. At about the same time, Giant, a bicycle manufacturer from Taiwan, China, entered the Chinese market. The two companies, which had a close relationship from the past, worked together to develop the high-end bicycle market for China. When Shimano entered the market, it supplied parts for bicycles that sold for roughly 200 yuan (Y), but it currently supplies parts mainly for bicycles in the Y 500–1,000 range. With its Kunshan factory operating over capacity, a second factory, in Tianjin, started production at the end of 2004.

Conclusion

At the end of *The Knowledge-Creating Company*, we noted that "[t]he essence of knowledge creation is deeply rooted in the process of building and managing syntheses" (Nonaka and Takeuchi 1995, p. 237). In particular, we emphasized the importance of synthesizing what appear to be opposites in order to create new knowledge organizationally in a spiraling manner. Seven syntheses are prerequisites to creating organizational knowledge.

1. Tacit and explicit
2. Body and mind
3. Individual and organization
4. Top-down and bottom-up (as management processes)
5. Hierarchy and task force
6. Relay and rugby (as metaphors for approaches to product development)
7. East and West

To create interorganizational knowledge—that is, knowledge across organizational boundaries—these syntheses are necessary but not sufficient. There must also be a synthesis of *inside and outside.*

Shimano has shown that interactions with the wide variety of outsiders with whom it forms vertical relationships (racers, consumers, retailers, and bicycle manufacturers), as well as outsiders with whom it forms horizontal relationships (universities, the local community, and even competitors) help to expand the knowledge spiral. In this regard, Shimano serves as a model of how companies should go about creating interorganizational knowledge through an *inside-outside* synthesis.

This chapter has emphasized the critical role *ba* plays in sharing, creating, and utilizing knowledge within organizations, as well as across organizational boundaries. *Ba* is conceptualized as an existential space in which inside and outside participants share their contexts and create new meanings through interactions. Shimano has created an ever-transcending knowledge ecosystem by multilayering various *ba* and expanding the existential space to a global scale. In this regard, Shimano is a model of how companies can go about developing interorganizational knowledge creation by synthesizing their various *ba* on a global scale.

References

Ahmadjian, Christina L. 2004. "Inter-organizational Knowledge Creation: Knowledge and Networks." In Hirotaka Takeuchi and Ikujiro Nonaka, editors, *Hitotsubashi on Knowledge Management*. Singapore: John Wiley & Sons (Asia).

Business Week. 2004. "The Tour de France's Other Winner." August 9.

Ishikura, Yoko. 2004. "Knowledge Management and Global Competition: Olympus's Approach to Global Knowledge Management in the Digital Still Camera Industry." In Hirotaka Takeuchi and Ikujiro Nonaka, editors, *Hitotsubashi on Knowledge Management*. Singapore: John Wiley & Sons (Asia).

Nihon Keizai Shimbun. 2004. "Kenmei ni Asobe [Play with Full Force]." January 28.

Nihon Keizai Shimbun. 2005. "Watashi no Rirekisho 22: Chugoku Seisan [My Personal History 22: Production in China]." July 23.

Nihon Keizai Shimbun. 2005. "Watashi no Rirekisho 26: Team Shimano [My Personal History 26: Team Shimano]." July 27.

Nonaka, Ikujiro, and Hirotaka Takeuchi. 1995. *The Knowledge-Creating Company.* Oxford University Press.

Shimano Inc. 2001. *Shimano 80 Nen-shi: 1921–2000 [Shimano's 80th Anniversary History: 1921–2000].* Shimano, Inc.

Shimano Inc. 2004. *The Shimano Story: Harmony and Strictness.* Shimano, Inc.

Takeuchi, Hirotaka, and Ikujiro Nonaka, editors. 2004. *Hitotsubashi on Knowledge Management.* Singapore: John Wiley & Sons (Asia).

Yamaguchi, Kazuyuki. 2003. *Shimano: Sekai o Seishita Jidensha Parts [Bicycle Parts that Won the World].* Kobunsha.

7

Creating the Dynamics of Hard-to-Imitate Innovation

Hirotaka Takeuchi

The increased competition faced by Japanese companies has produced a new think- ing about innovation. Realizing that traditional categories of knowledge were no longer enough, they have reconsidered long-standing habits and sought new mean- ings, fresh ways of thinking about innovation, and a new sense of direction. The economy's stagnation added to the urgency.

Although the 1990s is called a "lost decade" by many observers, even casual familiarity with leading Japanese firms shows that many made significant advances even while struggling with the decade's disruptions. Japan's capacity to turn a chaotic situation toward new knowledge creation has been displayed twice before: during the 1970s oil shocks and after the 1985 yen shock.

When the price of crude oil quadrupled in 1973, Japan's economy went into a recession that lasted four years. But the first oil shock was the catalyst for Japan's global leadership in energy conservation, which has benefited many industries. It triggered extraordinary upgrading as companies invested heavily in energy-con- serving technologies and moved toward higher-value products. The shock was also the impetus for the innovations that established Japanese firms in advanced indus- tries such as automobiles and consumer electronics.

The yen shock was the yen's 100% appreciation in the two years after the Plaza Accord of September 1985. Japanese products became expensive in inter- national markets. Wages (measured in U.S. dollars) reached some of the highest levels in the world, a sharp reversal for an economy where low wages relative to the West for skilled workers had been an important competitive advantage. Faced with such severe pressures, Japanese companies improved productivity enormously, shifting production of less sophisticated, lower-value products to overseas locations and moving to products less susceptible to price competition.

Although by no means as acute as the oil shock and the yen shock, Japan has been mired in seemingly endless stagnation and deflation since the collapse of the asset (stock and property) "bubble" in 1990. The economy has muddled through several recessions. There was a severe banking crisis. (However, since mid-2005 there have been signs of a recovery that may well prove sustainable.)

In these adverse circumstances, the Japanese companies studied in the previous chapters realized they had to go beyond cost reduction and conventional product upgrading. Instead, they involved their entire organizations in rethinking innova- tion itself. They sought to develop products, services, and systems that are hard to imitate by others.

This chapter reviews "what" kind of hard-to-imitate innovations Seven-Eleven Japan (SEJ), Toyota, Keyence, Nintendo, Sharp, and Shimano were able to develop, and examines "how" the innovations were developed.

Hard-to-Imitate Innovation

In the 1970s and 1980s, Japanese companies set the world standard for innovation centered on operational effectiveness—that is, for simultaneously improving quality and lowering cost. This includes such things as total quality management, *kaizen* (continuous improvement), *kanban* (just-in-time inventory), lean production, cycle time reduction, best practices, benchmarking, and supplier partnerships, among others. In many industries, compared to Western competitors, Japanese companies were able to maintain a formidable competitive advantage on both cost and differentiation.

Starting in the mid- to late 1980s, however, the gap in operational effectiveness with Western companies began to narrow. U.S. companies, in particular, began to imitate Japanese operational practices and pushed the productivity frontier even further ahead, especially through the use of information technology. (The productivity frontier is the maximum buyer value that a company can deliver at a given cost, using the best available technologies, skills, management techniques, and purchased inputs.)

Companies in other Asian countries also became able to imitate those operational improvements involving widely applicable management techniques, process technologies, and input improvements. Furthermore, even when Japanese companies developed more sophisticated product varieties, competitors within Japan and outside rapidly matched them, leading to competitive convergence. Firms came to realize that innovating on operational effectiveness and product upgrading alone does not lead to sustainable competitive advantage.

New thinking on innovation was in order. The companies featured in the previous chapters realized that the path to gaining sustainable competitive advantage was to push the entire organization to seek innovations that are not easily susceptible to imitation by competitors. This rethinking enabled them to move away from products and services that were being turned into commodities and onto new pathways to growth.

What the Firms Have Done

The case-study companies show that hard-to-imitate innovations come in different forms and shapes. Creating a new market is difficult to imitate for competitors (as SEJ has shown). So is establishing a trusting and loyal relationship with dealers (Lexus), making technological development a "black box" (Sharp), competing on the basis of invisible and nondimensional value (Keyence and Nintendo), and offering an integrated system of components to riders (Shimano).

Whatever form or shape it may take, companies can accrue clear-cut benefits from hard-to-imitate innovation. At a minimum, it leads to operational improvement and product upgrading. Beyond that, it can

- reduce the risk of a company falling into the commodity trap,
- raise willingness to pay on the part of customers, and
- direct companies onto a new pathway of growth.

Combining these, it can help companies achieve superior profitability. Thus, a survey of the case-study firms shows that all achieved above-industry profitability levels over the five years 1999–2003. SEJ's average ROIC was 16.1% points higher than for the Japanese convenience store industry as a whole. For Shimano's Bicycle Components Division, it was 16.3% points higher than the bicycle components industry average.[1]

Hard-to-Imitate Innovations Are Based on Tacit Knowledge

Innovation is a highly subjective process of personal and organizational self-renewal, requiring the personal commitment of employees as well as their identification with the company and its mission. It is not simply about putting together diverse bits of data and information.

Innovations are hard to imitate when they are based on tacit knowledge rather than on explicit knowledge. Explicit knowledge is expressed in words and numbers, and thus is easily communicated and shared in the form of data, formulas, or codified procedures. This makes it an easy target for imitation.

Tacit knowledge, on the other hand, is highly personal and hard to formalize, and thus is difficult to codify, communicate, or share. Subjective insights, intuitions, and hunches fall into this category. In addition, tacit knowledge is deeply rooted in an individual's action and experience. It encompasses the kind of informal and hard-to-pin-down skills captured in the term "know-how." A master craftsperson acts instinctively, almost automatically, and is often unable to articulate the scientific or technical principles behind the skill. Tacit knowledge is also deeply rooted in the ideals, beliefs, values, and emotions an individual embraces.

The Japanese approach to innovation is more heavily based on tacit knowledge than on explicit knowledge. It should be noted, however, that an overreliance on tacit knowledge can prevent the SECI process from taking place. The interaction of tacit and explicit knowledge is necessary for new knowledge to be created.

As an example, at Shimano, top management accumulates tacit knowledge from direct experience. The tradition dates to when Yozo Shimano mountain-biked down Mount Tamalpais in a business suit, completely staining the trousers with mud. This hands-on experience gave him valuable insights into a completely new type of bike that defied the conventional wisdom of how a bike is supposed to perform.

---

1. The primary profitability index used is return on invested capital (ROIC). Company-wide data were compiled for single-business companies such as SEJ. Divisional data were compiled for a division of multiple-business companies, such as the Bicycle Component Division of Shimano. Due to the proprietary nature of the dataset, disclosure of our findings is only for winners of the Porter Prize—SEJ and Shimano's Bicycle Component Division (1998–2002 data.)

The Porter Prize is an annual award bestowed on companies or divisions that have achieved above-industry profitability over an extended period and implemented strategies that are different from other competitors. It was started in 2001 and is organized by Hitotsubashi University Graduate School of International Corporate Strategy. The award is named for Professor Michael E. Porter of Harvard University, a leading strategy expert. More details on the Porter Prize can be found at http://www.porterprize/org/.

Rethinking the Innovation Process

Innovation is a management process. That is not to say happenstance and happy accidents will not continue to provide new products but, by their nature, they have never been methodologies a firm can rely on to remain competitive. By the end of the 19th century, German companies were systematically utilizing science to revolutionize the chemical industry and Edison was establishing a research laboratory. Under this approach, innovation meant developing new technologies in the lab, designing a product in-house, producing it at low cost, and tossing it at consumers.

But that is no longer necessarily the best way. Rather, today, many of the best innovations come from observing and interacting with customers to discover what they want, forming alliances with suppliers and retailers, and pulling in universities, communities, and even competitors. The environment has become much more open and collaborative. In other words, the process requires the involvement of a lot of people, both *within* and *outside* the company in what is being called the networked society. (For an excellent description of the trend toward "collaborative open-sourcing development" and "virtual commons" see Hof 2005.)

The case studies provide examples of leading-edge thinking on how to manage an innovation process today. They include:

- Setting lofty goals or driving objectives to align everyone in the organization toward a common direction ("reduction of lost opportunities" at SEJ).
- Creating a culture of "relentless pursuit of perfection" in which everyone itches to make improvements (Lexus).
- Sending top executives into the field to test new ideas and concepts (mountain bikes at Shimano).
- Knocking down organizational walls between R&D and manufacturing to enhance cooperation and collaboration (the Kameyama plant at Sharp).
- Forming cross-functional and cross-divisional project teams to build collective knowledge (advanced color display development at Sharp).
- Tapping the tacit knowledge of customers to develop fresh products and services (SEJ).
- Sending salespeople to customer production floors to hammer out solutions (Keyence).
- Peering over the shoulders of customers to discover what they are truly seeking (Nintendo).
- Sharing norms and values with independent dealers to gain their personal commitment and dedication (the Lexus Covenant).
- Reaching outside the company to link with scientists and overseas labs (Shimano).

Innovation requires collaboration, cooperation, interconnectivity, exchanges, and networking among the participants. The next sections describe "who" these participants are and "where" these interactions take place.

Innovation Requires Many Participants

The case studies make clear that innovation is not the doing of the selected few—a specialist in R&D, an engineer tucked away in isolation, or a marketing genius—but of everyone in the organization.

In the case of SEJ, frontline employees play a key role in bringing about hard-to-imitate innovation. Despite the extensive role of information technology in the convenience store industry, SEJ operations are largely based on the power of human insights. Even part-time workers are expected to think and act based on their own insights. Employees build their own hypothesis on how product will sell every time they place an order. For example, circumstances such as weather, road construction, and local activities such as festivals or sports events are taken into account. The company has created a special category of young employees, called *burabura sha-in* (walking-around employees), who wander around the stores and socialize with customers. The objective: bring in new insights, especially from young customers.[2]

At Keyence, innovations often come from the hands-on experience of salespeople who proactively head for the production floors of customers. They spend hours observing the manufacturing lines to gain insights into customer problems. Keyence's strength lies in sweating the details, continually hammering away at problems, and managing the thousand and one small insights gained on the customer's floor. With some 7,000 salespeople visiting 50,000 customers, these small insights lead to a large accumulated base of tacit knowledge.

Participants involved in the innovation process come from both inside and outside the company. Participants inside the company can be individuals, working groups, project teams, or informal circles. They are from diverse backgrounds, functions, divisions, and organizational levels. Participants from outside the company can be customers, suppliers, dealers, competitors, universities, local communities, or governments. They bring their individual contexts, share their contexts with others, and create new meanings through interactions among themselves, as well as with the environment. Through these interactions, which take place in an open environment but at a specific time and space, participants and the environment change, and so do contexts and meanings. This change in contexts and meanings enable new knowledge to be created from existing knowledge.

Types of *Ba*

The concept of *ba* is presented in chapter 1 and is referred to in the case studies. This section provides examples of the three types of *ba:* internal, external with customers, and external with noncustomers. (See Table 1.3 for a full characterization of *ba.*)

Internal Ba

An internal *ba* is one in which participants share their contexts and create new meanings through interactions among themselves.

Team or project members create new points of view through dialogue. Because individuals from different functions, divisions, and backgrounds are assembled together, this dialogue will contain considerable amounts of conflict,

---

2. Tactics such as *burabura sha-in* (and Shimano's caravans discussed in chapter 6) may contradict operational efficiency. It is very difficult to know in a quantifiable way whether the results "justify" the costs. Often, the benefits come from avoiding costs or making mistakes. That is, the interactions lead to understanding of what to avoid doing, change, or discontinue.

disagreement, and contradiction. It is precisely this *dialectic* perspective that pushes team members to question existing premises and to make sense of their experience in a new way. This kind of dynamic interaction within task forces and project teams facilitates the transformation of personal knowledge into organizational knowledge.

To gain a more concrete understanding of internal *ba,* consider two examples.

Sharp:
- Cross-functional task-forces assigned to strategically important product development projects, known as Urgent Project Teams;
- A joint project team drawn from television development engineers at one location and the LCD development engineers based at another site, to develop an advanced color display; and
- The Kameyama plant, where the television development department and the LCD technology development department colocated themselves, as an internal ba to produce next-generation television sets.

SEJ:
- Regular weekly meetings at its Tokyo headquarters attended by operation field counselors and headquarters staff, including the CEO, where tacit knowledge on better ways to provide services is shared;
- Weekly all-day meetings where managers seek to anticipate trends based on their tacit knowledge, often through context-specific metaphors; and
- Regular visits to distribution centers by distribution officers from headquarters, where problems are addressed and knowledge is shared face-to-face.

These meetings and visits are a *ba* because they are dynamic: contexts are shared and new meanings are created. A meeting in which most attendees remain silent does not constitute a *ba.* Nor does a data-dump type of meeting where explicit knowledge (bits of data and information) alone is shared qualify as a *ba.*

External **Ba** *with Customers*

An external *ba* is one in which participants inside an organization share their contexts and create new meanings through interactions with participants outside the organization.

Creating new meaning is not simply a matter of processing objective information *about* customers, suppliers, dealers, competitors, local communities, and other outside participants, as well as the environment surrounding them. Nor is it simply a matter of exchanging objective information *with* them. The case studies show that companies also have to mobilize the tacit knowledge held by customers. Indeed, most customer needs are tacit, which means the customers themselves cannot tell exactly or explicitly what they need or want. Some examples illustrate this.

Keyence uses the factory floor of its customer as an external *ba* to uncover the latent needs of the small and medium enterprises that make up the bulk of its clientele. Customers generally cannot specify the problems exactly, instead resorting to statements such as "make inventory management a little more efficient at the shop-floor level." Keyence salespeople spend long hours at the factory, investing in sharing contexts, which ultimately allows them to define both the problem and a solution.

SEJ uses its stores as an external *ba* to create new knowledge through face-to-face interactions with customers. Long-term experiences in dealing with customers give store employees unique knowledge and insight into their customers and their local market. Many of the experienced hands at SEJ say that they can just "feel" or "see" how well certain items will sell in their stores, although they cannot explain why (Nonaka and Toyama 2004, p. 104).

Nintendo has used the marketplace as an external *ba* to gain insights into what users find fun, surprising, emotionally compelling, and boring. No words are exchanged, only observations on how customers move their controllers wherever they may happen to be.

External **Ba** *with Noncustomers*

There are outside participants besides customers with whom companies interact. These include suppliers, dealers, competitors, local communities, and governments.

SEJ works closely with outside vendors and suppliers to codevelop original products through what is called "team merchandising." The external *ba* consists of team projects in which open knowledge sharing with outside vendors and suppliers takes place. The most intensive knowledge sharing takes place at sessions where vendors bring samples, recipes, and other embedded know-how to develop and improve various prototypes of a new product.

Lexus has made the frequent personal visits to dealers by executives from headquarters and the U.S. sales subsidiary an external *ba*. This philosophy enables both the automaker and dealers to come to grips with reality. In addition, Lexus uses a variety of meetings as an external *ba* in which contexts are shared and new meanings are created. They include a variety of meetings and advisory councils. One of the most intensive of these is the Fireside Chat, in which exchanges are made on a face-to-face and "gloves-off" basis (that is, without any restrictions).

Knowledge Ecosystems

A knowledge ecosystem is an extensive and interconnecting configuration of all three types of *ba*. Shimano has created one, and the concept is covered in chapter 6.

Managing *Ba*

To be good at managing *ba*, companies must ensure that the following five enabling conditions are met:

- Requisite variety: Participants from a variety of backgrounds, functions, divisions, management levels, organizations, industries, countries, and the like are interacting with each other.
- Dialogue: Participants need to actively engage in a free flow of ideas, express their subjective feelings, and share their personal experiences. They cannot be onlookers or bystanders.

- Dialectics: Participants need to embrace conflicts, contradictions, and dualities (explicit and tacit, subjective and objective, internal and external, etc.). Dialectic perspective pushes them to question existing premises and to make sense of their experience in a new way.
- Openness: Relationships need to be open, which requires the willingness on the part of participants to put aside preconceived notions. Membership is not fixed; participants come and go.
- Action-in-motion: When contexts, relationships, and the environment are in constant motion, they should serve as a trigger for companies to question their fundamental ways of thinking, seek new meanings, and take action to shake up long-standing habits and routines.

Implications for Developing Countries

The economic stagnation of the 1990s and early 2000s forced Japanese companies to question existing premises and shake up long-standing habits. This adversity served as a trigger to rethink innovation itself, with an eye toward developing products, services, and systems that are hard for others to imitate. Taken positively, a crisis situation increases tension within the organization and focuses the attention of members on defining the problem and developing solutions. The Japanese companies studied saw that contexts, relationships, and the environment were changing, and set out to renew themselves. Although the task was extraordinarily difficult, what they did seems quite simple in hindsight. They came to grips with ever-changing reality by engaging everyone in the organization, as well as those outside, and they made innumerable small innovations in a continuous and serial manner.

The Japanese experience since 1990 teaches a number of valuable lessons, many of which are relevant to developing economies. In particular, the experience has four implications for how developing economies can achieve a sustainable competitive advantage in the knowledge economy.

First, the key driver of growth is innovation. To promote growth and to avoid simply being another producer of commodity products, firms need to tap into "the growing stock of global knowledge" held by other firms, customers, members of the distribution chain, universities and research centers, consultants, competitors, local communities, governments, and a host of others outside the organization.

Although the focus in this book has been on hard-to-imitate innovations that occur "where the action is" on a day-to-day basis, and are based on tacit knowledge, they are often the precursor to scientific and technological innovations. For example, a new way of thinking about mountain bikes led Shimano to technological breakthroughs. Needless to say, both types of innovations are important. Developing countries have the advantage, even as latecomers to the knowledge economy, of being able to tap both types of innovations on a global scale.

Second, tapping into the growing stock of global knowledge is relatively easy in today's open and connected world. The psychological and technical barriers associated with sharing knowledge have come down dramatically as networks have become the locus for innovation. More than a billion people are linked online worldwide, creating what has come to be known as "virtual commons." This unprecedented shift in the environment is making it easier for firms to carry out collaborative open-sourcing development projects, forcing the walls across firms to come down and making the firms themselves more porous.[3]

Third, the management of innovation requires the involvement of everyone in the firm. Frontline workers, middle managers, and senior managers all play important but different roles in the middle-up-down management process, a Japanese-developed approach to knowledge creation mentioned in chapter 1.

Having a basic education system anchored in high standards has been a source of strength for Japanese companies. Developing nations must develop their education systems in order to participate in the knowledge economy. After all, companies do not innovate; people do.

Fourth, a large number of incremental adjustments and reforms affecting Japan's economic and institutional regime have taken hold since the 1990s bursting of the asset bubble. These changes include:

- Consolidation of industries
- Rise in corporate profits and dividend payout
- Change in ownership patterns (cross-sharing down, foreign ownership up)
- Increased mobility of the labor market and changes in employment law
- Overhaul of commercial law
- Change in accounting standards
- Amendments to antitrust law and increased power of the Fair Trade Commission
- Increased emphasis on corporate governance and enhanced role of outside directors
- Birth of the Financial Services Agency
- Opening of over-the-counter markets for equities
- Increased number of mergers and acquisitions
- Arrival of investment funds and partnerships
- Willingness to use the courts as arbiters in corporate disputes

Partly as a result of these changes, entrepreneurship is beginning to flourish within the Japanese economy. Rakuten, eAccess, Askul, and other start-ups are becoming main players on the Japanese business scene. In this regard, the Japanese experience in the last 15 years sends a clear message to developing economies: improve the economic and institutional context in order to stimulate knowledge creation and entrepreneurship. Getting the economic and institutional regime in order is a prerequisite.

On the competitive playing field an educated and skilled population is the player. The other pillars of the knowledge economy—the economic system, institutional regime, information infrastructure, and innovation system—are the field (or *ba*, to use our parlance).

Conclusion

It has been known since publication of *The Knowledge-Creating Company* in 1995 that Japanese companies are good at creating new knowledge intraorganizationally. The case studies in this volume show that Japanese companies are also good at creating new knowledge interorganizationally.

---

3. The spread of Internet connectivity has created concern regarding a "digital divide." This relates to the availability of information and communication technology, which refers to Internet access and computers generally. World Bank data show that the poorest countries, especially those in Sub-Saharan Africa, continue to lag.

It has also been known for some time that knowledge is created through the SECI process, which takes place both intra- and interorganizationally. The case studies show the role *ba* plays within the process. *Ba* provides the existential place where the individual conversions (socialization, externalization, combination, and internalization) are performed, where contexts are shared among the participants, and where new meanings are created.

For the management of innovation to succeed, execution is equally, if not more, important than strategy. Success requires *both* execution *and* strategy. The ability to embrace what can appear to be opposites has been at the core of management thinking since the phrases "the genius of the *and*" and "the tyranny of the *or*" were coined by Collins and Porras (1994, p. 45).

To succeed in today's knowledge economy, organizations need to embrace and synthesize syntactic opposites that are pieces of more comprehensive wholes. Tacit knowledge has to be shared with participants *both* inside the organization *and* outside the organization. Firms need to tap *both* tacit *and* explicit knowledge, embrace *both* internal *and* external *ba,* and focus on *both* micro (individual) *and* macro (environment). Knowledge is created dynamically by synthesizing these pairs. Thus, the key to leading the knowledge-creating process is dialectical thinking, which passes through a thesis-antithesis-synthesis spiral. (For further discussion, see Takeuchi and Nonaka 2004, pp. 1–27.)

The same can be said of the innovation management process. A synthesis of both order (thesis) and chaos (antithesis) has been instrumental in the continued international competitiveness of many Japanese firms. After all is said and done, putting this kind of thinking (dialectics) into practice may be the most difficult thing for others to imitate.

References

Ahmadjian, Christina L. 2004. "Inter-organizational Knowledge Creation: Knowledge and Networks." In Hirotaka Takeuchi and Ikujiro Nonaka, editors, *Hitotsubashi on Knowledge Management.* Singapore: John Wiley & Sons (Asia).

Collins, James C., and Jerry I. Ponas. 1994. *Built to Last.* New York: Harper Business.

Hof, Robert D. 2005. "Power of Us: Mass Collaboration on the Internet Is Shaking Up Business," *BusinessWeek,* June 20: 73–82.

Ishikura, Yoko. 2004. "Knowledge Management and Global Competition: Olympus's Approach to Global Knowledge Management in the Digital Still Camera Industry." In Hirotaka Takeuchi and Ikujiro Nonaka, editors, *Hitotsubashi on Knowledge Management.* Singapore: John Wiley & Sons (Asia).

Nonaka, Ikujiro, and Hirotaka Takeuchi. 1995. *The Knowledge-Creating Company: How Japanese Companies Create the Dynamics of Innovation.* Oxford University Press.

Nonaka, I., and R. Toyama. 2004. "Knowledge Creation as Synthesizing Process." In Hirotaka Takeuchi and Ikujiro Nonaka, editors, *Hitosubashi on Knowledge Management.* Singapore: John Wiley & Sons (Asia).

Shimano Inc. 2004. *The Shimano Story: Harmony and Strictness.* Shimano, Inc.

Yamaguchi, Kazuyuki. 2003. *Shimano: Sekai o Seishita Jidensha Parts [Bicycle Parts that Won the World].* Kobunsha.